SPURGEON
ON
REVIVAL

SPURGEON ON REVIVAL

A BIBLICAL AND THEOLOGICAL APPROACH

by
ERIC W. HAYDEN

WIPF & STOCK · Eugene, Oregon

Wipf and Stock Publishers
199 W 8th Ave, Suite 3
Eugene, OR 97401

Spurgeon on Revival
A Pattern for Evangelism Today
By Hayden, Eric W.
ISBN 13: 978-1-5326-4626-3
Publication date 12/27/2017
Previously published by Zondervan Publishing House, 1962

CONTENTS

Introduction 9

I. The Surrey Gardens Music Hall Ministry 25

II. The Revival of 1859 39

III. What Spurgeon Wrote About Revival 53
    His Published Works

IV. What Spurgeon Said About Revival 67
    Post - 1859 Sermons, Speeches and Addresses

V. What Spurgeon Preached During the Revival Year.. 85

   A. Divine Election 89

   B. Human Depravity 97

   C. Particular Redemption 108

   D. Effectual Calling 116

   E. Final Perseverance 128

Addendum to Chapter II 139

Postscript 143
    Wherein Arminian and Calvinist Agree

INTRODUCTION

INTRODUCTION

A great spiritual awakening, or revival of true religion, is urgently needed in our time. Denominational statistics alone impress this upon us — closed churches, diminishing memberships, a catastrophic decline of Sunday school scholars, the lack of regular conversions and baptisms. These alone ought to make us realize that nothing less than Almighty God stepping in and bringing about a revival of true Christianity will remedy the situation.

The moral and spiritual degeneration of the world points to the same thing: broken marriage relationships, juvenile delinquency, overcrowding of our prisons (two or three men to a cell where there should be only one); the police trying to combat gang warfare in many of our towns and now easier and more open facilities for betting; the continued toll of death upon our roads through drunkenness; the illegal traffic that is always going on in drugs. These are further indications that point to the need of revival. Because the church has been so inadequate to meet this twentieth century moral and spiritual decline, what is needed is a heaven-sent revival. It is most heartening that this is being recognized by all the denominations. Many now have their revival fellowships, although they may be called by another name. They are putting out literature explaining the need; half-nights or whole nights of prayer are being organized. That is not to say that this is the way to arrange for a revival to come; it is only an indication of the burden, the yearning, the interest, the earnestness in many people's hearts of all denominations. Not only so, but our religious printing presses are producing works dealing with revival. Old classics have been reprinted like Arthur's *Tongue of Fire*. New works on revival like *In the Day of Power* by Arthur Wallace are being issued — or the several books describing the Irish revival of 1859. There are more and more books and literature of all kinds being printed because this great need is being felt.

We have at last seen that all the new methods which have been urged upon us have made no appreciable effect upon the masses. C. H. Spurgeon used to tell of a little "backwoods" Christian community in the United States. The membership of the church was declining so the group had a meeting and said that if only they bought a new chandelier the whole village would come to see it. The first Sunday after its installation the building was crowded, but the following Sunday they were back to the usual few — the chandelier had been seen — it was not worth coming for a second look! The moral is plain. We have relied upon movies and filmstrips. We have had all the advantages that audio-visual aids may offer us, but the result is almost negligible for the simple reason that what the church is trying to do is to put on a kind of show that the world can do and usually much better. The churches are not going to draw the ordinary person who watches the television screen, or who has been watching the cinema screen for ten or fifteen years. They are not going to flock into the churches to see a second-rate Christian film — Christian film producers just do not possess the money; they do not have the actors, and so it is no good saying, "Anything the world can do, we can do better" — we cannot. The world can outstrip us. The evangelistic film ministry is rapidly on the decline. No longer do the Billy Graham films which have been greatly used bring in the crowds that they once did.

What is needed, then, is a real Holy Spirit revival. Of course, sometimes we use other alternative terms. Often we speak of revival, but sometimes we speak of a spiritual awakening. Perhaps really we ought to use the word revival, because it is a Biblical word. It occurs sixteen times in the Word of God, fourteen times in the Old Testament and twice more in the New Testament. Why is it not more of a New Testament word? For the simple reason that New Testament Christianity is revived Christianity. The letters of the apostle Paul are written to a people who are in a revived state. In actual fact the two places in the New Testament where it is used, it is not used in the sense in which we are using it here.

Two examples of the word in the Old Testament are: Psalm 85:6 where the Psalmist cries out, "Wilt thou not revive us again; that thy people may rejoice in thee?" The Hebrew word, "revive," here means to make alive, to recover, to repair, to restore, to make something whole again that has been split up into pieces. It is used also in Habakkuk 3:2, a great heart-rending cry from the prophet, "O Lord, revive thy work in the midst of the years." Again it is this same Hebrew word. The equivalent word in the New Testament is the word that is used by Paul in II Timothy 1:6, "Wherefore I put thee in remembrance that thou stir up the gift of God which is in thee, by the putting on of my hands." The Greek word, "stir up," means to fan into flame, to revive. Thus you see how this is a great Biblical word, and in our English language according to the Oxford Dictionary it has come to mean "a reawakening of religious fervor."

Here is the answer to the moral and spiritual decline of our world. Here is the answer to the religious situation in the churches of all denominations — a reawakening of religious fervor brought about by God's Holy Spirit.

There are, however, those who prefer the term, "spiritual awakening." What they imply by these words is renewed vitality for the churches, renewed vigor and power in preaching, a direct intervention of God the Holy Spirit upon His own people. There is justification for using such a term, although it is not Biblical language, for spiritual awakening is precisely what happened, for instance, in Acts 2:17. You will remember that was Peter's explanation in his sermon on the Day of Pentecost of what had just happened — there had been a spiritual awakening, God had fulfilled the prophecy of Joel and had poured out His Holy Spirit upon all flesh, and that is something which God has done repeatedly through the centuries. Some people mistakenly call this "a baptism of the Holy Spirit." It is not a baptism, for the Holy Spirit at Pentecost was "poured out" upon. A baptism is "immersion into." We are baptized by the Holy Spirit at conversion; when we are regenerated, we are "baptized into Christ." We also experience as Christians, the filling of the Holy Spirit, when He fills us for special forms of service. Sometimes we experience the anointing of the Holy Spirit, but above and beyond this experience there is something which the Bible knows as an outpouring of the Holy Spirit, more than we have ever experienced at conversion or for sanctification, or for Christian service. There is a further blessing which God is ready to bestow in His own sovereign time. He can shower down upon His people His Spirit, and that is what people mean when they speak of a spiritual awakening or a religious revival.

Throughout the centuries, God in His sovereignty has been pleased to visit His church in such a way. We see it first of all in the Bible. In both the Old and New Testaments there are records of such revivals. Outside of Bible history such spiritual awakenings have occurred in almost every century under such men as Luther, Knox, Whitefield, Wesley, etc., and of course they have occurred in almost every part of the world, in India, in the Outer Hebrides, in Wales, in Ireland, in England, in Ruanda and in many places too numerous to mention, but it is now over 100 years since revival visited England, for example. In 1859 when revival came to this country C. H. Spurgeon himself was experiencing revival blessing, and in the same year he was laying the foundation stone of the Metropolitan Tabernacle. Thus we are going to try and discover the secret — or the secrets — of the revival which visited this land and in which Spurgeon himself played such a big part.

First we must note that God, although He is sovereign and can do all of His work Himself if He wishes, uses men. It is true to say that in every revival there is a "revivalist," although the word is unfortunate in that it makes us think of a kind of roaming evangelist, exhorting men and women to "work-up" a revival. Nevertheless, in every revival there seems to be at least one man — sometimes a group of men — whom it pleases God to deign to use and bless. Before we start saying that there is no Spurgeon alive today or begin to pray, "O God, send us another Spurgeon," let us note what Dr. John Macbeath has said: "God never repeats Himself."[1] Wesley was not a repetition of George Whitefield. Spurgeon and Moody were distinct individuals, they were not a copy of a previous man, and today God can take any one of us and act upon us and through us to bring about revival. God used Spurgeon 100 years ago, and in the introduction to his volume of sermons printed at the end of 1859, the great preacher wrote: "The times of refreshing from the presence of the Lord have at last dawned upon our land. Everywhere there are signs of aroused activity and increased earnestness. A spirit of prayer is visiting our churches, and its paths are dropping fatness. The first breath of the rushing mighty wind is already discerned, while on rising evangelists the tongues of fire have evidently descended."[2]

Of his own particular church he went on to say, "For six years the dew has never ceased to fall, and the rain has never been withheld. At this time the converts are

[1] In a personal conversation with the author (1/11/59): Minister's Vestry, The Metropolitan Tabernacle.
[2] *The New Park Street Pulpit* (London, 1859), p. v, Preface.

more numerous than heretofore, and the zeal of the church groweth exceedingly."³

We have there the clue to revival under C. H. Spurgeon. It was not merely an accompaniment or an outcome of the American revival of 1857 — that that revival came to these shores and influenced Spurgeon. Spurgeon points us back six years: before the revival had even occurred in America. In his autobiography, complied by his secretary and his wife, we have the record of that six years prior to the revival reaching England. Spurgeon said: "When I came to New Park Street Chapel it was but a mere handful of people to whom I first preached, yet I could never forget how earnestly they prayed. Sometimes they seemed to plead as though they could really see the Angel of the Covenant present with them, and as if they must have a blessing from him. More than once we were all so awe-struck with the solemnity of the meeting that we sat silent for some moments while the Lord's Power appeared to overshadow us; and all I could do on such occasions was to pronounce the benediction, and say 'Dear friends, we have had the Spirit of God here very manifestly tonight; let us go home and take care not to lose His gracious influence.' Then down came the blessing; the house was filled with hearers, and many souls were saved."⁴

There is not a single biography of Spurgeon that mentions these words, but how important they are! No assessment of the secret of Spurgeon can ever be made without taking them into account. Some people have tried to explain the secret of Spurgeon's power and have talked about his eloquence, or his secret as being his own prayer life; or they tell the story of how he would take people downstairs to the Tabernacle's basement lecture hall where the prayer meeting was held saying, "Here is our power house." The secret of the revival blessing that attended Spurgeon's

³ *Ibid.*
⁴ *Autobiography,* Vol. 1, p. 360.

INTRODUCTION 15

ministry was not in 1859, the secret is found six years previously in that little New Park Street Chapel, Southwark. Spurgeon and his group of members had a Holy Spirit Pentecostal experience, and the divine unction came down upon the young preacher.

He had an experience comparable to John Wesley's heart-warming experience, or one similar to D. L. Moody's "accolade of fire,"[5] as it is called, which the American evangelist experienced in November, 1871. A man named Moorhouse told D. L. Moody how deficient he was of the Holy Spirit, especially in his preaching. Then there were two women who dogged Moody at all the gatherings (he called them "those Dreadful Women"!) and they kept coming up to him and saying, "You haven't got it yet."

C. H. Spurgeon's experience was also similar to that of the revivalist Charles Finney when he knelt in a wood and seemed to be surrounded by the presence of God. I wonder if we have become afraid of undergoing such an experience ourselves today? It is a shattering experience physically. Some men have felt as if they were going to drop dead when this experience came upon them, but they said afterwards that they would never go back again to what they were before.

The preface to the 1859 volume of sermons explains how the revival continued: "Sound doctrine and loving invitation make a good basis of material, which, when modelled by the hand of prayer and faith, will form sermons of far more value in the saving of souls than the most philosophic essays prepared elaborately, and delivered with eloquence and propriety."[6] Thus the revival continued because of "sound doctrine" and "loving invitation" and in the Preface to the volume he mentions some of the sermons in that revival which God signally blessed. "Compel Them to Come

[5] Day, R. E., *Bush Aglow* (Philadelphia, 1936), p. 127.
[6] *The New Park Street Pulpit* (London, 1859), p. v, Preface.

In" — Spurgeon wrote that no week went by without conversions coming from the reading of it. Others were: "The Shameful Sufferer," "The Blood," "Faith in Perfection," "The Bed and Its Covering," "Mr. Fearing Comforted," "Who Can Tell?," "Come and Welcome," and "The Chaff Driven Away."

Let us notice that his emphasis was upon sound doctrine first of all, for it was against unsound doctrine that he was to take a lonely stand later on. He warned the Baptist Union in after years that what we now call "modernistic tendencies" were creeping into the denomination, and later events proved how right he was. Prosperity and progress soon became after his death spiritual decline. Many people concentrate on the point, "Was he right or was he wrong in leaving the Baptist Union?" That is not the important question, but: Was he right or was he wrong in making a protest at all? And surely statistics prove that he was right.

There are some statistics in *A Short History of the Baptist Union*[7] and of course, the author, being the secretary of the Union, seeks to prove that Spurgeon was wrong in leaving the Baptist Union. The statistics given by Dr. E. A. Payne proved beyond a shadow of doubt that Spurgeon was absolutely right in his protest. The statistics are for five-yearly intervals. The year of the great Down Grade Controversy was 1887, C. H. Spurgeon died in 1892. A wave of progress continued for a number of years after his death, which is easily explained by the fact that he was instrumental in founding about 200 churches in the Greater London area and the home counties, and men were still going out from his College with the sound doctrine that Spurgeon himself preached. Then we notice from the statistics that in 1911 the decline began to set in. Although there were more churches than in Spurgeon's day (in fact 95 more churches) there were 16,133 fewer members, and there had been a loss of 14,491 Sunday school scholars. In

[7] *Op. cit.*, pp. 267, 268.

1957 although there were still more churches, 525 more Baptist churches than in Spurgeon's day, there were only 24,433 members, and 145,998 Sunday school scholars had been lost! No wonder this landslide is described by E. J. Poole-Conner in his book *Evangelicalism in England*, as "floodtide and ebb."[8] Spurgeon had made his protest. He had warned them of what would happen if the sound doctrine was not preached.

While many today say that the neglect of the prayer meeting is our trouble and others that the church is old-fashioned, not "geared to the times," offering us better publicity and advertising as the solution — surely the secret is to return to the Biblical doctrines proclaimed by C. H. Spurgeon.

There is an interesting passage written by Spurgeon when he says quite definitely that he has discovered in the revivals of the past a close vital connection between doctrine and revival:

> In the history of the church, with but few exceptions, you could not find a revival at all that was not produced by the orthodox faith. What was that great work which was done by Augustine, when the church suddenly woke up from the pestiferous and deadly sleep into which Pelagian doctrine had cast it? What was the Reformation itself but the waking up of men's minds to those old truths? However far modern Lutherans may have turned aside from their ancient doctrines — and I must confess some of them would not agree with what I now say — yet, at any rate, Luther and Calvin had no dispute about Predestination. Their views were identical, and Luther's *Bondage of the Will* is as strong a book upon the free grace of God as Calvin himself could have written. Hear that great thunderer while he cries in that book, "Let the Christian reader know, then, that God foresees nothing in a contingent manner; but that He foresees, proposes, and acts, from His eternal and unchangeable will. This is the thunder stroke which breaks and overturns Free Will." Need I mention to you better names than Huss, Jerome of Prague,

[8] *Op. cit.*, p. 176.

Farel, John Knox, Wickliffe, Wishart and Bradford? Need I do more than say that these held the same views, and that in their day anything like an Arminian revival was utterly unheard of and undreamed of.

And then, to come to more modern times, there is the great exception, that wondrous revival under Mr. Wesley, in which the Wesleyan Methodists had so large a share; but permit me to say that the strength of the doctrine of Wesleyan Methodism lay in its Calvinism. The great body of the Methodists disclaimed Pelagianism, in whole and in part. They contended for man's entire depravity, the necessity for the direct agency of the Holy Spirit, and that the first step in the change proceeds not from the sinner, but from God. They denied at the time that they were Pelagians. Does not the Methodist hold, as firmly as ever we do, that man is saved by the operation of the Holy Ghost, and the Holy Ghost only? And are not many of Mr. Wesley's sermons full of that great truth, that the Holy Ghost is necessary to regeneration? Whatever mistakes he may have made, he continually preached the absolute necessity of the new birth by the Holy Ghost, and there are some other points of exceedingly close agreement; for instance, even that of human inability. It matters not how some may abuse us, when we say man could not of himself repent or believe; yet, the old Arminian standards said the same. True, they affirm that God has given grace to every man, but they do not dispute the fact that apart from that grace there was no ability in man to do that which was good in his own salvation. And then, let me say, if you turn to the continent of America, how gross the falsehood that Calvinistic doctrine is unfavourable to revivals. Look at that wondrous shaking under Jonathan Edwards, and others which we might quote. Or turn to Scotland — what shall we say of M'Cheyne? What shall we say of those renowned Calvinists, Dr. Chalmers, Dr. Wardlaw, and before them Livingstone, Haldane, Erskine, and the like? What shall we say of the men of their school but that, while they held and preached unflinchingly the great truths which we would propound today, yet God owned their word and multitudes were saved. And if it were not perhaps too much like boasting of one's own work under God, I might say, personally, I have never found the preaching of these doctrines lull this church to sleep, but ever while they have loved to maintain these truths they have agonised for the souls of men, and the 1,600 or more whom I have myself baptized, upon profession of their faith,

INTRODUCTION 19

are living testimonials that these old truths in modern times have not lost their power to promote a revival of religion.[9]

That, of course, was not only Spurgeon's emphasis; it was the emphasis in the New Testament. Peter's sermon on the day of Pentecost was a doctrinal sermon. There was one sermon Paul preached on Mars Hill when he was not doctrinal, and there was little result from his preaching, but when Paul was doctrinal then revival blessing came. The converts on the day of Pentecost "continued in the apostles' doctrine"; Timothy was urged to "pay attention to doctrine," elders, said Paul, were to "labour in the word and doctrine" and "by sound doctrine both to exhort and to convince."

Today's Christianity by contrast is superficial; there is little doctrine, little theology in it. We have been suspicious of it because of higher criticism, or we have thought it was too learned to be imbibed by simple people, and so we have given people a sort of "easy-believism" gospel. One hundred years have gone since Spurgeon preached his doctrinal sermons, and there has been no great national revival developing into an international awakening since. There have been local ones as on the Isle of Lewis, but no great national revival since Spurgeon's doctrinal sermons of 1859. Why is it? Spurgeon lived in days similar to our own. He lived in days that may be described as scientific days. The Darwinian theory of evolution was gaining interest and had taken a hold upon some people's minds. There was the invention of the telegraph system; and G. M. Trevelyan calls the period "The Railway Age."[10] Spurgeon was living in days of scientific achievement, and yet there was moral and spiritual degeneration as there is today. We are living, then, in precisely the same kind of situation: intellectual and philosophical achievement, sci-

[9] *The New Park Street and Metropolitan Tabernacle Pulpit* (London, 1861), pp. 302, 303 — Exposition of the Doctrine of Grace given by C. H. Spurgeon during the opening meetings of the Metropolitan Tabernacle.
[10] Trevelyan, G. M., *English Social History* (London, 1942), p. 531.

entific discovery and advancement, and yet moral and spiritual decline and no revival. The modernist, or liberal theologian, claims to have found a new approach to the Bible and to have liberated hundreds from a blind belief in inspiration. Dr. W. B. Glover writes: "There is little reason to believe that evangelicalism could have survived the nineteenth century without it [belief in inspiration] as anything more than an out-moded religious anachronism confined to uneducated obscurantists and irrelevant to the main stream of Western civilization."[11]

He believes that the modernist has liberated the man in the street from trying to believe in an inerrant Bible; perhaps he has, but what has he given him in its place? There was a time when a man believed that the Bible was the Word of God, and what have we been given in its place? Nothing! And so we are living in days when the church is not a power to be reckoned with; when our politicians want to altar the Sunday observance, or make betting and gambling easier, they feel quite at ease in doing so for the churches themselves have "thrown away" the authority and inspiration of the Bible.

Certainly we have evangelism today. We have churches where the way of salvation is presented after a fashion and decision for Jesus Christ made easy. We have a kind of fashionable youth rally now and again. That is not to say that some of our modern evangelism has not had results, but are these results comparable to those of 100 years ago? Surely we must get back again to where Spurgeon was. Those of us who are preachers need to repent; we must confess to God and before others that we have gone wrong. It is said that in his later years Spurgeon mellowed — a misleading term, for the next step after mellowing is that fruit rots! It may be that Spurgeon altered the style of his preaching, or that he altered his presentation of his sermons

---

[11] *Evangelical Nonconformists and Higher Criticism in the 19th Century* (London, 1954), p. 287.

in the way that the style of Shakespeare's earlier plays are different from his later plays.

Toward the end of his life Spurgeon was asked to revise some of his earlier sermons for publication. He wrote: "I was happy to find that I had no occasion to alter any of the doctrine which I preached in those earlier days of my ministry . . . as to the truths themselves, I stand just where I did when the Lord first revealed them to me."[12] He did not "mellow." The doctrines he proclaimed at the end were the doctrines he proclaimed at the beginning. The doctrines he proclaimed even from his death-bed were the doctrines he preached in New Park Street Chapel, and also those he preached with such power in the Surrey Gardens Music Hall in 1859.

Are we not justified then in turning to these sermons which fell with such power on the ears of the hearers and resulted in such blessing? May it please the sovereign God of revival to deal with preachers and hearers today that we may see revival in our time.

[12] *Autobiography*, Vol. 2, p. 158.

THE SURREY GARDENS
MUSIC HALL MINISTRY

I

THE SURREY GARDENS MUSIC HALL MINISTRY

C. H. Spurgeon began his ministry in the New Park Street Chapel in 1854. Before twelve months had passed the Chapel needed enlarging to accommodate the many people who wanted to hear him. The deacons and Spurgeon found that by incorporating the vestries and school halls into the sanctuary of the church, and then by building new Sunday school halls along one side with sliding partitions they would be able to accommodate larger congregations. During these alterations to the Chapel in New Park Street, services were held in the Exeter Hall, Strand, but when the New Park Street Chapel was reopened it still proved to be too small. It was like attempting, said Spurgeon, "to put the sea into a teapot." They had, in fact, wasted their money — they had enlarged their premises, but still they could not accommodate all the hearers who desired to come. Hundreds were being turned away, the streets were blocked every Sunday, and those inside the church nearly suffocated from the heat. Again within twelve months it was resolved by the church that Exeter Hall should be booked for regular Sunday evening gospel services, at least during the summer months. But the hall was inconveniently situated for a man whose ministry was to a population south of the river. The proprietors were also loath to rent the Exeter Hall to one denomination regularly. And the Hall was too small! Meanwhile the idea had gradually developed in

Spurgeon's mind that a special structure, "the largest Chapel in the world," must be built, and so a fund was started for what was later to become the first Metropolitan Tabernacle — the foundation stone of which was laid in 1859 and the opening performed in 1861.

Spurgeon's attention had been drawn to a newly-erected music hall in the Royal Surrey Gardens. In these grounds were fountains, caves, summer houses, walks and lawns, a lake and even a menagerie — and beside all these amenities, if we can call them such, there was a building which seated between ten and twelve thousand people. We must not imagine it was a music hall in the sense of the term used today, that is, for vaudeville shows, etc. The Surrey Gardens Music Hall was used for orchestral concerts and for operatic works. Even so the opponents of Spurgeon said that he should not preach in such a temple of worldly amusements. Undeterred by his opponents, Spurgeon with Deacon Olney went to look over the music hall, and seeing its three galleries and realizing the great possibilities in every way for his Sunday evening services, booked the hall for Sunday evening, the 19th of October, 1856, and the three successive Sunday evenings.

Spurgeon is called "the Innovator" by one of his biographers — J. C. Carlyle. He declares that Spurgeon was a man before his time — and in many of his ways he was, especially regarding his hiring of the Surrey Gardens Music Hall. Today it is quite common to read of meetings of an evangelistic nature in public buildings, in town halls, football stadia, sports arenas, and who knows where else. But here again we notice Spurgeon's emphasis. He said: "We did not go to the Music Hall because we thought it was a good thing to worship in a building usually devoted to amusement, but because we had no other place to go."[1]

There are various societies and movements that say that if they hold an evangelistic youth rally, it must be on

[1] *Autobiography*, Vol. 2, p. 199.

THE SURREY GARDENS MUSIC HALL MINISTRY 27

neutral territory. There must be no denominational bias; it must be in some place where outsiders will be attracted. Well, if this is the proper thing to do, let us stop building churches and erect more club halls! Spurgeon, however, was a man who believed in Church-building and in building churches! He believed in preaching a Gospel that would build up the Church of Jesus Christ, and he believed in erecting churches for that special, God-ordained ministry.

Nevertheless, it was the only thing that was expedient at that time, and so the Surrey Gardens Music Hall was engaged for this Sunday night evangelistic ministry. As soon as the step was taken and it was known, there was a clamor for tickets. Tickets were issued the members and congregation of the New Park Street Chapel and the public had to get in without. The streets were thronged and it was a most un-nerving sight for Spurgeon when he first tried to enter the music hall. Not only was the building filled, but there were 10,000 people in the grounds hoping to get in. There were between two and three thousand people in the passages in the building. There were others looking in through the windows; the orchestra pit was filled with people. Nothing like it had been seen before. George Whitefield and John Wesley had assembled crowds equally great, but that had been in the open air. There had never been such an indoor meeting for the worship of God and the proclamation of the Gospel. There is, however, only one word with which to describe that first service in the Surrey Gardens Music Hall — and it is the word "disaster."

The service proceeded in quite an orderly fashion until Spurgeon began what we term "the long prayer" — and then some conspirators shouted out: "Fire"; others are said to have shouted: "The galleries are giving way," and immediately there was a resistless wave of people seeking to get out. Some, knowing that they would be the last out of the doors, leapt from the gallery and the result was a large number of casualties. Naturally Spurgeon tried to preserve order and calm from the pulpit. When quietness was restored he sought to close the service, but there were cries of "Go on — preach." He gave a short message from Proverbs 3:33 — "The curse of the Lord is in the house of the wicked." A hymn was sung, and the people were dismissed.

The effect upon Spurgeon can hardly be imagined. It is said in most of the biographies that his mind was in danger of becoming unhinged. He was led out of a back door — he did not see the seven dead bodies laid out on the ground. Neither did he know for some time of the twenty-eight injured. It was suggested to the police that perhaps the conspirators were thieves, but after their close investigations, the police did not think so. There were, of course, pickpockets who took advantage of the commotion and confusion, but on the whole the police thought it must have been personal enemies of Spurgeon and the evangelical doctrine that he was proclaiming. He himself said later of the catastrophe:

> On a night which time will never erase from my memory, large numbers of my congregation were scattered, many of them wounded and some killed, by the malicious act of wicked men. Strong amid danger, I battled against the storm; nor did my spirit yield to the overwhelming pressure while my courage could reassure the wavering, or confirm the bold; but when, like a whirlwind, the destruction was overpast, when the whole of its devastation was visible to my eye, who can conceive the anguish of my sad spirit? I refused to be comforted; tears were my meat by day, and dreams my terror by night.
>
> ... Then came the "slander of many" — barefaced fabrications, libellous insinuations and barbarous accusations. These alone might have scooped out the last drop of consolation from my cup of happiness; but worse was to come, and the utmost malice of the enemy could do no more.
>
> ... On a sudden, like a flash of lightning from the sky, my soul returned to me. The burning lava of my brain cooled in an instant. The throbbings of my brow were still; the cool wind of comfort fanned my cheek, which had been scorched in the

furnace. I was free, the iron fetter was broken in pieces; my prison door was open, and I leaped for joy of heart.[2]

Twenty-five years after the disaster, the author of one of the biographies of Spurgeon, Robert Shindler, met Spurgeon when he was preaching at the Baptist Union meetings in Portsmouth. Every seat in the hired hall was occupied; many people were standing; and there were hundreds still pressing to get in. When Spurgeon reached the platform and saw what was before him, Shindler said he was nearly unmanned and stood in the passage leaning his head on his hands. He preached but could not entirely recover from the agitation.

William Williams, who wrote *Personal Reminiscences of C. H. Spurgeon,* and who was very friendly with the great preacher, once told Spurgeon that on the following day he (Williams) was going to preach from Proverbs 3:33. Spurgeon said: "That is the very text I had on that terrible night of the accident at the Surrey Gardens Music Hall," and he spoke the words with a deep sigh and a blanched countenance.

Immediately after the accident Spurgeon retired to a friend's house in the country, and there came the day when he had a sudden realization that Christ was stronger than the devil, and then he had renewed joy of heart and was able to resume his ministry at New Park Street. The proprietors of the Music Hall refused to take any fee for the disastrous evening, and as the building had been engaged for four consecutive Sundays they allowed him to preach there for four Sundays running, beginning on November 23.

Before resuming at the Surrey Gardens Music Hall, Spurgeon preached to a great congregation at Whitefield's Chapel in Tottenham Court Road (it was the chapel's centenary). His theme there was revival, and he preached

[2] *Autobiography,* Vol. 2, pp. 195-196. Quotation from *The Saint and His Saviour.*

on Habakkuk 3:2, "O Lord, revive thy work in the midst of the years, in the midst of the years make known; in wrath remember mercy."

The first Sunday in the Music Hall there were only 8,000 in attendance. That was not surprising. The police had seen to it that greater precautions were taken. The management had insisted that instead of an evening service he must preach in the mornings, because the authorities felt it would be safer than the darkness of evening-time. The following announcement was made: "It is proposed to hold a service here on the three following Sunday mornings. It is much to the inconvenience of my congregation to attend here. We have a comfortable place of worship elsewhere. There we are happy together; there I have a congregation and as many members as any mortal man can desire. It is only with a view of winning souls to God that we have come to this larger place, and should we be accused of other objects the judgment-day will lay bare what our motives have truly been."[3]

These Sunday morning services continued throughout 1857. Who can imagine the physical strain on the preacher's voice and also on his nervous system? Besides preaching to these vast audiences he had many other commitments. He was usually preaching four or five times during the rest of the week in different parts of the country, appealing for funds for the Tabernacle he hoped to build. It was the Music Hall ministry, however, that became one of London's chief attractions. These services were attended by nobility and royalty, from the Prime Minister on down. "At no time have so many of the aristocracy made acquaintance with Nonconformist worship."[4] Statesmen, nobles, divines, travelers, explorers, artists, actors, authors, they all came and sat at the feet of the prince of preachers. Seats had to be taken by 10 o'clock in the morning by ticket holders. At 10:30

[3] Pike, Vol. 2, p. 254.
[4] *Autobiography*, Vol. 2, p. 222.

the door was open to non-ticket-holders. More than 1,000 people were normally turned away every Sunday. The year 1858 was the year of revival in America, but in one "Life" of Spurgeon it is stated: "And some awakening at home, especially in connection with the continued services of Mr. Spurgeon at the Surrey Gardens."[5]

One of the most important works on revival in recent years is Dr. J. Edwin Orr's *The Second Evangelical Awakening in Britain*. He estimates that the revival that came to America in 1857, spreading to Ireland, Scotland and Wales, and finally to England, did not reach Southern England and London till 1860, or the summer of 1859 at the earliest. Dr. Orr states that "Spurgeon was at the height of his power as a preacher in London whilst the revival meetings were in full swing."[6] But Spurgeon was experiencing revival blessing three years before 1860; indeed, it began six years prior to the Surrey Gardens ministry, when they had the wonderful prayer meetings in the New Park Street Chapel. While preaching in the Music Hall in 1859 Spurgeon said, "Can you recollect how you prayed that . . . God would yet fill this place with His glory? And do you remember how long ago that is, and how God has been with us ever since?"[7] That is revival. When people pray desperately for a manifestation of God in His glory, God comes into the midst of His people and does not leave them.

But the secret was not only prayer. As we have already seen, Spurgeon associated doctrinal preaching with revival, and in the Music Hall in 1858 this is what he said:

> When first I preached in this hall . . . I was then simply an evangelist, preaching to many who had not heard the Gospel before. By the Grace of God the most blessed change has taken place; and now, instead of having an irregular multitude gathered together, my congregation is as fixed as any minister's in the

[5] Pike, Vol. 2, p. 290.
[6] *Op. cit.*, p. 190.
[7] *Autobiography*, Vol. 2, p. 221.

whole of London. . . . From being an evangelist, it is now my business to become your Pastor in this place. . . . Now, since the circumstances are changed, the teaching will be changed also. I shall not now simply confine myself to the doctrine of faith or the teaching on believer's baptism; I shall not stay upon the surface of truth, but shall venture, as God shall guide me, to enter into those things that lie at the basis of the religion that we hold so dear. I shall not blush to preach both the doctrine of God's divine sovereignty; I shall not hesitate to proclaim, in the most unreserved and unguarded manner, the doctrine of election. I shall not be afraid to propound the great truth of the final perseverance of the saints; I shall not withhold that undoubted teaching of scripture, the effectual calling of God's elect.[8]

That is precisely what he did. From a study of the sermons preached in the revival year of 1859 we shall see that he kept to his word. In the last service he conducted in the Music Hall before he entered his own Tabernacle, he took as his text Acts 20:26, 27, "Wherefore I take you to record this day, that I am pure from the blood of all men. For I have not shunned to declare unto you all the counsel of God." And that well summarized his three years' ministry in the Surrey Gardens Music Hall. He had given the people doctrinal sermons, and the result was revival blessing.

For three years he maintained that revival ministry. It was a one-man ministry. Dr. Billy Graham and others have filled larger places, but for shorter periods. Today's evangelists have a team behind them. Here was a ministry sustained for three years by one man in a building that accommodated between ten and twelve thousand people, and the emphasis was upon doctrinal evangelism resulting in the visible building up of the Church of God. There were indeed many striking conversions.

Spurgeon often gave his congregation some Holy Spirit-inspired sallies and thrusts; and once in the Music Hall he pointed and said, "There is a man sitting there, who is a shoemaker; he keeps his shop open on Sundays, it was open

[8] *Autobiography*, Vol. 2, pp. 223, 224.

last Sunday morning; he took 9d, and there was 4d profit; he sold his soul to Satan for 4d."⁹

There actually was a shoemaker present, and he *had* kept his shop open, and he *had* taken 9d, and he did make a profit of 4d — *and* he was converted. Dozens were converted like this and joined the church.

What can we learn from this amazing ministry? Is there any abiding message? Is there some Biblical or theological truth that we must take hold of today when we so desperately need revival?

We have already touched on the connection between sound doctrine and evangelism resulting in revival, and we shall see more of that as we study the content and character of the sermons preached during 1859 in the Music Hall. Is there not a lesson to be learned from the very disaster that occurred on the first occasion when Spurgeon preached there, for he himself often used that disaster as a lesson.

We cannot help relating the catastrophe to the incident recorded in Acts 19. In the commentary by the late Dr. Campbell Morgan we read: "The victories in Ephesus did not satisfy the heart of the apostle. From the midst of abundant and victorious labour he looked on over the whitened fields of harvest until his gaze rested in strong desire upon the central city of earthly power, and he said, 'I must also see Rome.' "¹⁰

If ever there was a man with a city's name engraved upon his heart, it was C. H. Spurgeon and London. He yearned over this city — we can best discover it in his prayers, in such a collection of his public prayers as that by Dr. C. T. Cook, or an older collection entitled *The Pastor at Prayer*. Time and time again he prayed to Almighty God and wrestled with Him for this sinful city of London. As

⁹ *Ibid.*, p. 226.
¹⁰ *The Acts of the Apostles* (London, 1924), p. 457.

Paul was concerned for Rome, so Spurgeon was concerned for London.

The uproar in Ephesus occurred because of a man called Demetrius. Dr. Campbell Morgan comments: "Demetrius gathered the craftsmen together, and told them what this man Paul was doing. This caused the disturbance, but the end was peace, patronage, and protection for the Christians."[11] Just as good came out of the evil of the uproar at Ephesus, so good came out of the disaster of the Music Hall in the Royal Surrey Gardens. As the Christians of Paul's day received patronage, so we have already seen there were many people, from royalty downwards, who patronized the Music Hall. Dr. Campbell Morgan says: "Vast crowds were gathered together for worship. The theatre into which they crowded, taking with them the two travelling companions of Paul, was capable of seating 20-30,000 people. These facts help us to understand the commotion of the city."[12] He was referring, of course, to the fact that when considering such a great number of people we have to think in terms of mass hysteria, and there is every evidence of that in the record of Acts 19. "Cheer leaders" organize encouragement for football teams, and that was the case in the stadium at Ephesus. For two solid hours they did nothing but chant "Diana of the Ephesians — Diana of the Ephesians." What a remarkable parallel there is. We are also told that "some cried one thing and some another."[13] To go back to the Music Hall — some cried, "Fire," some cried, "The galleries are giving way"; the place was in uproar, but out of it all came peace, prosperity and patronage.

It was of course the silversmith's speech that explains all. Vested interests were at stake. Paul had not made any outspoken attack on the little silver images of Diana of the Ephesians — he had merely preached the Gospel. But when the Gospel is preached, and men and women are saved,

[11] *Ibid.*, p. 458.
[12] *Ibid.*, p. 459.
[13] Acts 19:32.

and their lives are changed, they realize that there are things that they must cease doing. Although there had been no direct attack upon the silversmiths and their craft, they were losing money because people did not want useless idols. So it was in the Music Hall ministry. Surely some of those who raised the false alarm were only afraid of their vested interests. Perhaps there were those who were in the liquor trade. Perhaps the formal religionists were there who did not want the living Gospel of Charles Haddon Spurgeon. These are the kind of parallels that there are between this uproar at Ephesus and the uproar at the Surrey Gardens Music Hall.

Then there is this lesson which Spurgeon himself drew from the accident: "I have many times used the great calamity as an illustration of the truth that accidents are not to be regarded as Divine judgments."[14] He used those words first of all in a sermon when there had been a terrible train disaster which occurred on a Sunday, and many Christian people affirmed it to be a judgment of God on Sunday travelers!

[14] *Autobiography*, Vol. 2, p. 214.

*THE REVIVAL
OF 1859*

II

THE REVIVAL OF 1859

Almost every book dealing with a spiritual awakening or a revival of history begins by describing the pre-revival situation in approximately the same words. For instance, you will read such words as these: "the darkness before the dawn"[1]; "the sleep of midnight and gross darkness"[2]; or "dissolution and decay."[3] W. T. Stead, who was a child of the Welsh Revival of 1859, when writing of the later revival in the principality of the twentieth century, said of it: "Note how invariably the revival is preceded by a period of corruption."[4]

The American revival of 1857, from which issued the awakenings in Ireland, Scotland, Wales and England a year or two later, was no exception. From 1845 to 1855 the religious life of the United States of America was in a serious decline. The contributing factors were these: great material prosperity had had a serious effect upon the Americans, widening the gulf between the "haves" and the "have-nots"; violent crimes had been on the increase with great rapidity; spiritualism had gained a popular hold over many minds; free love was being advocated and accepted by many; corruption was rife in the commercial and the political life of the nation; the laws of the land still legalized the cruel

---
[1] Hood, E. P., *Vignettes of the Great Revival* (London, 1856), p. 9.
[2] Rees, E. E., *Christmas Evans*, p. 9.
[3] Poole-Connor, E. J., *Evangelicalism in England* (London, 1951), p. 1.
[4] *The Revival in the West* (London, 1904), p. 14.

system of Negro slavery. Atheism, agnosticism, apathy and indifference to God, to the churches and their message, abounded on every hand. The decline then was a four-fold one — social, moral, political and spiritual; and of course we are seeing something similar in our own day. The accumulation of wealth has become easier, and we are living in what could be called "boom times," and as so often happens, the morals of the people are degenerating. When people begin to think money can buy them anything; that once they have accumulated sufficient money, then they will have the home they want, and that money will bring the pleasures they want; when they begin to make a god out of money and out of luxuries, and are gripped by the spirit of greed and materialism, then we find that they have no time for God. The church and the Christian message is relegated to a lesser place or discarded altogether.

In America there came a great awakening in 1857 — an awakening to the situation, the decline and the corruption in which they found themselves; and that was followed quickly by a great spiritual awakening. Banks and business houses failed, factories and railways closed down, vast numbers were soon unemployed, and it needed the quietness of shut-out industry and transport in order for a nation to hear the still small voice of God! In 1857 God spoke to America — and to London two years later.

America began to live again — live spiritually, from North to South, and East to West. Millions of converts were added to the churches of all denominations. And what proved the genuineness of the revival was the ethical result, for the social effects of the revival continued for almost half a century.

Geographically the blessing spread to Great Britain, covering every county. Numerically, over a million converts were added to the churches in England. Evangelistically, the Kingdom of God was extended through the upsurge of new movements and societies, such as The Salvation Army, the Children's Special Service Mission, the China Inland Mission. Socially, a large number of philanthropic societies concerned with the welfare of children or the reclaiming of prostitutes and alcoholics, or the rehabilitation of criminals — these societies developed and prospered. The same thing could happen again within twelve months. Once more we have come to a dreadful spiritual decline and corruption of morals. Conditions in the world are very similar to America over 100 years ago, and Great Britain, too, at that time.

But besides the prevailing pre-revival conditions which we have already mentioned, the revivals of history all stress the importance of the prayer meeting, united prayer meetings, Christians of all denominations meeting together. These have always paved the way for a revival. The revival of 1857 in America and 1859 in Great Britain was no exception. Here it is impossible for us to separate revival personalities from these pre-requisites of revival, and we must begin with a New York business man named Jeremiah Lanphier — who gave up his business in order to become a city missionary. He had not been a city missionary long before he sent out an advertisement for a noon-day prayer meeting to be held on Wednesdays in the Dutch Church at the corner of Fulton Street in downtown New York. This man went to the room that he had hired. Five, ten, fifteen, twenty, twenty-five minutes went by, and no one turned up, until after he had waited half an hour, six others came one after the other. They prayed, and the next week there were twenty, and the famous Fulton Street prayer meeting had begun. The first week in October it was decided to hold the meeting daily instead of weekly, and within six months 10,000 business men were meeting every day to pray for revival. Within two years a million converts had been added to the American churches.

Ireland was the first European country to be affected by this awakening. In 1856 a Baptist lady called Mrs.

Colville did a great deal of personal work, testifying and witnessing to the power of Jesus Christ in her own life. She greatly influenced a young man named James McQuilkin of Ballymena. He was converted and a few days afterwards saw a book in a shop about George Müller of Bristol. He bought the book. He read it, and there was created in his heart a great soul-hunger for a like-minded friend with whom he would be able to pray. He wanted a spiritual companion in the way, and God sent him one, and these two prayed again, and the two became four. Every Friday they met for prayer in a school house near the village of Kells; and they were meeting during the same month that the business men were meeting at Fulton Street, New York.

The news of the United States revival had not yet reached Ireland. When it did reach Ulster in 1858, the Presbyterian Church of Ireland sent observers to America to see what was going on. They came back thrilled by what they had observed. One of them wrote an influential book which was circulated among the ministers of Ireland. Many ministers began to preach about revival, and strangely their prayer meetings began to multiply. Not only did the attendance grow in the one prayer meeting they had, but other prayer meetings had to be held, and already they were experiencing revival in their midst in this village of Kells. One of the group was a young man called Samuel Campbell, and he went to his home which was some distance away and there was greatly used to the conversion of his family as well as some friends and neighbors. The whole group then began to meet in a Presbyterian church. The crowds were too great for them to be accommodated, so they spread out to other villages; and then from the villages of Ireland the flame spread to towns like Belfast and Dublin and Cork: all were affected by the revival.

What of Scotland? Again the American news created great interest in Scotland. Prayer meetings were organized in Edinburgh, Glasgow and Aberdeen, so much so that the

United Presbyterian Church reported in 1859 that one in four of their communicant members was attending a regular prayer meeting, and that there were 129 new prayer meetings started. Revival first broke out in Aberdeen as the result of a united prayer meeting in the county buildings. Scores of people, sometimes up to a hundred, were converted every night in that prayer meeting. That is one of the features of this 1859 revival — that conversions not only took place in church services, but they took place actually in prayer meetings. Sometimes the prayer meetings were held in the street, a school playground, or a public house, and there were conversions! News of the Irish awakening, of course, brought further interest to Scotland. Glasgow especially was prayed for specifically, and soon revival broke out there. It spread across the water to the Isle of Bute, Rothesay being visited by an evangelist called Brownlow North. Then it spread to Dumbartonshire, Renfrewshire, Lanarkshire, eventually permeating every corner of Scotland.

At that point Wales came under the Holy Spirit's influence, until every county in the principality knew of the awakening. A Welsh lad named Humphrey Rowland Jones had been turned down by the Wesleyan District Meeting when applying as a candidate for the Methodist ministry. He emigrated to America to seek training there. Completing his theological course, he was ordained to the Methodist ministry in America. In the American revival in 1857 he became a revivalist preacher, and he returned to his home, Wales, in 1858. A neighboring minister, David Morgan, at first distrusted Humphrey Jones and his revival emphasis. The strange thing is that David Morgan was himself a product of revival, a minor one that had occurred in Cardiganshire in 1841. He overcame his prejudices, went to hear the young revivalist from America, and entered into a deep spiritual experience. Together they began to pray and work for a spiritual awakening in Wales, until Jones became rather unbalanced and faded out of the picture altogether and

Morgan was on his own. But David Morgan was used to spread the genuine revival to the neighboring villages, until the whole of Cardiganshire was revived. From the South it spread to Montgomeryshire, and then it spread still further afield. One after another instance is recorded of the way being prepared through united prayer meetings, many of them attended by only two or three. Thus Carmarthenshire, Radnorshire, Glamorganshire – and soon all the principality felt the fire.

Finally England was reached. In August, 1859, a united prayer meeting was held in the throne-room of the Crosby Hall, a wide invitation throughout the Metropolis having been issued. It attracted both the "white-collar" and the manual worker. Within a month 100 people were meeting at noon for prayer. At the beginning of October there were 6 daily prayer meetings and several weekly ones. By the end of the month, the paper called *The Revival* (now *The Christian*) was listing 9 daily and 16 weekly prayer meetings. In November the numbers had grown to 20 daily and 40 weekly and in December there were 24 daily and 60 weekly. A few days later 120 prayer meetings were reported in London until finally the editors of the paper ceased from publishing a detailed list, because the number had grown so great.

The awakened Christians in London sought ways and means of extending the blessing they were experiencing. They were helped by a notable man, the Seventh Earl of Shaftesbury, who made it possible for religious meetings to be held in theaters by sponsoring the Religious Worship Act. In the new year of 1860, the Fortune, the Garrick, and the Sadler's Wells Theatres were open for Sunday evening services. Special services were also held in St. Paul's Cathedral and Westminster Abbey. Spurgeon, however, was already experiencing revival blessing following a prayer meeting at Park Street Chapel – he was conducting services in the Music Hall, the Royal Surrey Gardens.

THE REVIVAL OF 1859

The blessing soon flowed to the districts of outer London and to the satellite towns in Kent and in Surrey. Prayer meetings were begun in Croydon in 1859. The blessing spread to Sussex and Hampshire, across the Spithead to the Isle of Wight. Berkshire had its revival prayer meetings in Reading around 1859. From Bristol it spread to the West Country; Gloucester and Wiltshire experienced the revival. Somerset towns were holding their prayer meetings, and in Dorset people were flocking to hear Evan Hopkins. Devon and Cornwall were not to be left out.

One would have thought that in a revival that began in Ireland and then spread to Scotland the flame would have tended to spread from the North to the South, but revival "has the sovereignty of God in it," as F. B. Meyer said, and you can never tell where it will break out next. We have already seen that it went from Ireland to Scotland, and on to London and the South. The flame then spread up to the Midlands; and the picture is not complete unless we just follow the course of the awakening. We are mostly concerned with London because of Spurgeon's ministry, but the revival spread from the Metropolis to the Midlands, by the way of East Anglia. Once more the united prayer meetings were the secret. The Universities of Oxford and Cambridge had special prayer meetings. From 1859 onward similar prayer meetings began in Bury St. Edmunds and Lowestoft. The counties of Hertfordshire, Buckinghamshire, Warwickshire, Northamptonshire, Huntingdonshire (here the American revivalist Charles Finney was responsible for an awakening in 1859), Worcestershire, Herefordshire, Shropshire and Staffordshire (where a localized revival occurred simultaneously with the American one of 1857), Leicestershire, Nottinghamshire, Derbyshire — all these counties experienced revival as the outcome of local prayer meetings in which Anglicans and Nonconformists seemed to play an equal part.

The main difference between the Irish, Scottish and

Welsh awakenings, and the London revival, was that in the first three it was more of a spontaneous and immediate type of revival running its course within a few months, but in the London revival it seemed to be more of a delayed action. Dr. J. Edwin Orr in *The Second Evangelical Awakening in Britain*[5] describes it as "an insemination period" of prayer meetings, followed by "an incubation period" when the curious and the spurious dropped away, and this was followed by "a period of evangelism"[6] when the real ingathering occurred as a result of the earnest intercessors who had redoubled their efforts after some in the middle period had dropped away.

The awakening in the North of England followed the spontaneous pattern of Ireland. In Northumberland it began by a visit of two Americans. From Newcastle upon Tyne it spread to other parts of Northumberland and Durham. In Cumberland it began with the visit of two Irishmen. Although sparsely populated, Westmorland experienced the same blessing as Cumberland. Lancashire and Cheshire were awakened, too, due to an upsurge of prayer meetings and the visit of Charles Finney to Bolton in 1859. The people of Yorkshire prayed for a revival in their united prayer meetings, and within six weeks God had answered their prayers.

Needless to say, as in all revivals, there was opposition, not first and foremost because of the doctrines proclaimed, but because of the physical effects — various physical phenomena. These surely are the things that make many people fearful of revival in our time. We shall see later what Spurgeon thought himself of all these so-called excesses and physical phenomena. We have all heard of people going into hysterics, prostrating themselves on the floor at prayer meetings; and we have been rather afraid that if we pray for revival we might have to go through similar distressing

---

[5] Much of the material for this chapter is taken from Dr. Orr's book, published by Messrs. Marshall, Morgan and Scott (London, 1953).
[6] *Op. cit.*, p. 147.

experiences. We say we are living in a cultured age, and we do not want to see men and women carried home in such a state as that. But in the revival of 1859 there were experienced leaders who laid a hand of restraint upon the emotional excesses, and of course we have to realize that this kind of emotional excess is not confined to evangelical Christianity and revival. The arrival of a film star, a thrilling race, an exciting football game, a brutal prize fight — all these are frequently the scenes of mass hysteria about which no one takes any notice whatever. But let us come down to specific examples; in America there did not seem to be many instances of physical phenomena publicized. Some newspapers did report that there was an unhealthy excitement — people sometimes made open confession of their sins before the rest of the prayer meeting, and that became a little bit contagious. There were indeed some who prostrated themselves on the floor in the prayer meetings. But these excesses seemed to be rare.

In Ireland there were one or two outstanding examples. For instance, there was the blasphemous boy who posted himself at the door and who mocked those going in with such obscene language that they were not surprised to see him struck down as if by lightning. For some hours he lay as if dead, but eventually he got up, requested prayer for himself, and was converted on the spot.

Criticism of the revival was more evident in Ireland than anywhere else, because of the great Roman Catholic population. The priests wrote and spoke about the "nervous diseases" of revival. They warned their people about the likelihood of convulsions, epilepsy and insanity. There were people who prostrated themselves; but those who wrote about it were careful to point out that it was not really hysteria, but rather a deep convicting work of God.

What of these conditions in Scotland, among the so-called "dour" Scots? Again there were some reports of prostrations, but it seems that the other physical phenomena were dispensed with. In Scotland God seemed to work in a much quieter way; people certainly were found in great distress in the streets and occasionally were flat on their faces.

The Welsh — unlike the Scots — are known for their emotional and excitable natures. Naturally there was far more singing in the revival in Wales than went on elsewhere. There was what some describe as "holy exuberance," there was a great deal of trembling and other signs of emotional distress. Dr. J. Edwin Orr tells of a Nonconformist wife who was taking her Anglican husband to a chapel revival meeting. He did not feel he would be able to sit right through such a noisy meeting, but halfway through nudged his wife and said, "I have got to shout!" She said, "You be quiet." A little later on he said, "But I must shout!" She replied, "Go back to your own church and shout there." A little later he said, "If I don't shout I shall die." "Well, shout then," she said, and being a good Anglican he stood up and shouted, "I believe in God the Father . . . — " and continued to the end of the Creed!

In England there was some emotional distress, though it was not that of hysterical girls, but "strong men bowed down" — strong men under a wave of conviction from God, prostrating themselves. And we must note that these manifestations gradually faded away after the early period of the revival. To those who may be afraid of revival today for this very reason, it seems as if God does away with the physical manifestations after they have served His purposes, just as in the New Testament days there were wonders, miracles, and signs that eventually passed away. So it seems that in a revival we have these startling excesses and physical manifestations at first only in order to arouse interest and to gain people's attention. Then, when the leaders have exercised restraint and God has quieted things down, these manifestations, which may be looked upon by others as counterfeit, fade away.

THE REVIVAL OF 1859

How are we to relate all this to the Word of God, making a Biblical and theological approach to the subject? We have stressed that the prayer meeting paved the way for a revival, and we read in II Chronicles 7:1, "Now when Solomon had made an end of *praying*, the fire came down from heaven, and consumed the burnt offering, and the sacrifices; and the glory of the Lord filled the house." And in verse 14 we read: "If my people, which are called by my name, shall humble themselves *and pray*, and seek my face, and turn from their wicked ways; then will I hear from heaven, and will forgive their sin, and will heal their land." If we are to relate it to the New Testament then we note Acts 1:13 and 14, "And when they were come in, they went up into an upper room . . . (and) all continued with one accord in prayer and supplication," and Acts 2:1, "They were all with one accord in one place, and suddenly there came a sound from heaven as of a rushing mighty wind, and it filled all the house where they were sitting."

Apart from the Old Testament and the New Testament examples we only have to look to ourselves. Christians of all denominations have to agree that one of the most tragic signs of twentieth century Christianity is the decline of the prayer meeting. Here surely is the main secret of revival: when once again we begin to take God at His word, when we realize that He is the sovereign God of revival and is waiting to be asked for it. He can send it when and where He wills, and through whom, but He is waiting until we earnestly gather together in prayer.

What of the theology of the revival in 1859? One account says: "The revival was seen at its greatest intensity among the traditionally Calvinistic denominations of Ulster, Scotland and Wales."[7] That is precisely what Spurgeon pointed out with great emphasis, that when Calvinistic doctrines are preached then they can be associated with a spiritual revival. Therefore there was nothing new in the

[7] *Ibid.*, p. 251.

theology of 1859. "All of its teachings were derived from the New Testament, and many of its strong doctrinal points were doctrines recovered in the Reformation."[8]

The hymnology of the revival also emphasized Calvinistic theology. The most popular hymn sung during the revival years was: "Lord, I hear of show'rs of blessing." The emphasis all the way through the hymn is upon the work of God in salvation: "Let Thy blessing fall on me," "I am longing for Thy favour," "Speak the word of power to me." There is nothing in that hymn about human effort. There is nothing about any self-works. The whole emphasis is on the sovereign grace of God, that He can, if He wills, pass us by, or on the other hand send a deluge of blessing. A hymn written in 1836 became popular in the revival of 1859. "Just As I Am" is a great hymn of human response, but again the emphasis is upon divine sovereignty: "And that Thou bidst me come to Thee"; "Thy love has broken every barrier down."

The emphasis then was on what God can do and has done. Another hymn popular during 1859 and later also had a Calvinistic emphasis. It was written in 1855 — "Oh, Happy day that fixed my choice." Again, although it is a hymn of human response, it also emphasized God's sovereignty in salvation: "He drew me, and I followed on." When we return to that emphasis which was the emphasis of Charles Haddon Spurgeon, combined with the re-emphasis of the prayer meeting, then we may expect God to revive us again.

[8] *Ibid.*, p. 252.

*WHAT SPURGEON WROTE
ABOUT REVIVAL*

III

WHAT SPURGEON WROTE ABOUT REVIVAL

HIS PUBLISHED WORKS

Spurgeon is referred to in most of the biographies as "a very prolific writer." There are, in fact, some 135 books that bear his name on the cover, and if we were to take into account some of the pamphlets and magazines that he also edited, the number could easily be raised to 200. Actually he wrote few books as books, and he confessed that he found it extremely hard work. In the preface to the first of his published volumes, *The Saint and the Saviour*, published in 1857 (the year that revival broke out in the United States of America), he wrote: "Writing is to me the work of a slave. It is a delight, a joy, a rapture to talk out one's thoughts in words that flash upon the mind at the instant when they are required; but it is pure drudgery to sit still and groan for thoughts and words without succeeding in obtaining them."[1] He went on to say that it was quite right to refer to an author's book as his "work" for that is what he found writing — hard work! It took him more than two years to write *The Saint and the Saviour*, and he declared that he only finished it through "a sense of duty."[2]

He quickly discovered that instead of writing specifically for publication, he could collect and revise passages from his own sermons, and put them together in book form for publication. We will not go so far as to say, as was

[1] *Op. cit.*, Preface, p. v.
[2] *Ibid.*

said of his predecessor at New Park Street Chapel, Dr. Gill, that he always preached with an eye to publication. Spurgeon did not preach that he might have his words in book form at a later date; but he did find that it suited him better to have a full-time secretary to collect material from his speeches, addresses and sermons, edit them in book form, and then all he had to do was to check the final proofs.

The only books that were written really as books were *The Saint and the Saviour, All of Grace, According to Promise, or Around the Wicket Gate, The Clue of the Maze, The Bible and the Newspaper, Eccentric Preachers,* and a few more slim volumes that nevertheless gained great popularity during his lifetime. Most of them were really only enlarged tracts setting forth the way of salvation for seekers after Jesus Christ, or explaining how young believers could be strengthened in their faith. Then there were one or two commentaries such as *The Gospel of the Kingdom,* his commentary on Matthew's gospel, republished by Zondervan in 1962 under the title, *Spurgeon's Popular Exposition of Matthew*), and of course *The Treasury of David,* his fine work on the Psalms. The remainder of Spurgeon's published works were collected sermons, speeches and addresses. And they, of course, supply us with an abundant amount of material for discovering what he *said* about revival.

Are we then left with little written evidence of Spurgeon's views upon revival? Only if we are going to confine our research to books that were written as books for evidence. Spurgeon, however, edited a monthly magazine, *The Sword and the Trowel,* which he established in 1865. He edited that magazine until the year of his death, 1892, and these volumes are practically untapped or untouched by research students who have desired to write a biography of Spurgeon or a history of his various institutions; and these old magazines are full of C. H. Spurgeon at his best. Of course, it is a Herculean task to read through 27 volumes to discover all that we would like to know about him, but the effort well repays the student of Spurgeon and revival.

First, however, in the group of books already mentioned, Spurgeon made some important statements concerning revival. Following the practice of John Newton, who declared that he read the newspaper that he might see how his Heavenly Father governed the world, Spurgeon so read his newspaper, and he took various interesting items from the newspapers of 1878 and commented on them in the light of Bible truth. They were then published in a slim volume entitled *The Bible and the Newspaper*, and in this book revival is alluded to several times. For instance, the prevalent fear of revival that we have touched on previously: the fear that religious people sometimes have of so-called excesses, prostrations, and mass hysteria and various other physical phenomena — Spurgeon had something to say on the matter.

On April 11, 1878, there was a great gale which resulted in floods in many parts of the country. The basement premises of the Tabernacle were flooded out, so that they could not be used for some time. Naturally this made Spurgeon think of God opening the windows of heaven in a spiritual sense and sending revival blessing, and so he wrote: "Every now and then this happens in spiritual affairs, and men behold the phenomenon with wonder and even alarm. It was so in the age of Whitefield and Wesley, when the Lord opened the windows of heaven upon our land. What an outbreak there was! What a commotion and upheaval! The old pavements of conventionality were torn away and the floods burst up through them."[3]

Commenting in the same volume on the *Daily News* description of the *Dreadnought*, the then "most modern battleship," Spurgeon wrote a chapter in *The Bible and the Newspaper* which he called "Life versus Machinery." He wrote: "We see this life and force breaking out in many

[3] *Op. cit.*, p. 43.

places in new works for the Lord Jesus, and frequently it takes very irregular forms, greatly to the distress of spiritual Tories, who must have all things cut and dried after the most ancient fashion. We confess that we, also, are somewhat perplexed at certain of the more outrageous forms of religious energy, but even if there should be occasional irregularity it is better than the monotony of mere mechanism."[4]

We have already seen that there is generally opposition to a revival. Spurgeon, commenting again on the flood incident, said, "Attempts were made to stop the stream: persecution was tried against the Methodists, they were denounced from the pulpit, threatened by mobs, and ridiculed as modern enthusiasts and madmen, and regarded as the offscouring of all things; but all this availed nothing, omnipotence was at work, and malice could not hinder."[5]

Although writing only nineteen years after the great revival year of 1859 in England, already Spurgeon saw the need for a further awakening. The churches had once more begun to put their trust in men, in methods and movements, in organizing ability and organizations, and so he cried out in *The Bible and the Newspaper:* "Are we not all in danger of trusting to religious machinery, and leaving the work of the Lord to be done by secretaries, committees, missionaries and so forth?"[6] He continued: "May the like happen again in our times; indeed, we are not altogether strangers to such burstings forth of the living waters even now."[7] While deploring the religious state of the land at large, he himself, nineteen years after the wonderful ministry in the Surrey Gardens Music Hall, was still experiencing the floodtide of revival.

It has been said that the reality of a revival can be tested "by its ethical results." What kind of social better-

[4] *Ibid.*, pp. 109, 110.
[5] *Ibid.*, pp. 43, 44.
[6] *Ibid.*, p. 108.
[7] *Ibid.*, p. 44.

ment does it bring in its train? What kind of new reform and legislation is passed as a result of the awakening? For Spurgeon that was the only satisfactory revival — one that had an ethical result. He wrote:

> It were well . . . that the Divine life would break forth everywhere — in the parlour, the workshop, counting-house, the market and the streets. We are far too ready to confine it to the channel of Sunday services and religious meetings; it deserves a broader floodway and must have it if we are to see gladder times. It must burst out upon men who do not care for it, and invade chambers where it will be regarded as an intrusion; it must be seen by wayfaring men streaming down the places of traffic and concourse, *hindering the progress of sinful trades* (author's italics), and surrounding all, whether they will or no. Would to God that religion were more vital and forceful among us, so as to create *a powerful public opinion on behalf of truth, justice and holiness*. . . . A life which would *purify the age*. It is much to be desired that the Christian Church may yet have *more power and influence* all over the world for *righteousness . . . social reform and moral progress*.[8]

That was revival for Spurgeon. He did not mind the excesses and physical phenomena, as long as they did not go beyond certain bounds. But the real test was: Did it bring about any moral and social progress as well as spiritual blessing?

From the volume, *The Gospel of the Kingdom*, Spurgeon's commentary on the gospel of Matthew, it is clear that Spurgeon had high hopes of revival crowds gathering beneath the gospel preaching. Commenting on Matthew 4:25, "And there followed Him great multitudes of people," Spurgeon wrote that, "It is a hopeful sign when there is a great enquiry after Jesus, and every region and city yields its quota to the hearing throng."[9]

His own personal longing for revival is expressed in a comment on the Lord's early days of ministry (Matthew

[8] *Ibid.*, pp. 44-46.
[9] *Op. cit.*, p. 20.

9:33), "O Lord, give the people around us to see such revivals and conversions, as they have never known before!"[10]

In *The Treasury of David* Spurgeon comments on Psalm 85:6, "Wilt thou not revive us again, that thy people may rejoice in thee?" He comments on that verse:

> We are dead or dying, faint and feeble, God alone can revive us. He has in other times refreshed His people, He is still the same, He will repeat His love, will He not? Why should He not? We appeal to Him — "Wilt thou not revive us again, that thy people may rejoice in thee?" A genuine revival without joy in the Lord is as impossible as spring without flowers, or daydawn without light. If, either in our own souls, or in the hearts of others we see declension, it becomes us to be much in the use of this prayer, and if on the other hand we are enjoying visitations of the Spirit, and the bedewings of grace, let us abound in holy joy and make it our constant delight to joy in God.[11]

There we see his expectation of future revivals. There too we see his emphasis upon prayer as efficacious in promoting a revival.

The pattern of *The Treasury of David* is: Spurgeon's notes, then comments made by Puritan commentators and others, followed by a pithy section which he entitled "Hints to the Village Preacher." In that section, on Psalm 85 he sums up verse six like this: "Revivals imply decline" (he is reminding us that the pre-revival situation is always declension or corruption in the moral, spiritual, commercial, industrial, political life of a nation); — "Revivals are from God"; "Revivals are frequently needed"; "Revivals are in answer to prayer"; and "Revivals are occasions for great joy."[12]. There we have a summary of C. H. Spurgeon's views upon revival. Revivals imply declension; revivals are from God — they are not worked up — they must be prayed down. Revivals are in answer to prayer, and revivals are occasions of great joy.

[10] *Ibid.*, p. 65.
[11] *Op. cit.*, Vol. 4, pp. 85, 86.
[12] *Ibid.*, p. 97.

In *The Sword and the Trowel* for December, 1866, Spurgeon wrote an article entitled, "What Is a Revival?" and the main points made there are illustrated by comments made elsewhere in the volumes of this magazine. First of all, he stated that "the word 'revival' is as familiar in our mouths as a household word. We are constantly speaking about, and praying for revival."[13] Would that could be said of more ministers and members of our churches! Revival was a household word; no wonder Spurgeon saw revival. He was continually speaking about it, praying for it, expecting it, creating a yearning and a longing in the hearts of his Tabernacle members for it — and they witnessed it. He explained in this article, "What Is a Revival?" that the word "revival" is one of Latin derivation meaning "to live again" or "to receive again a life which has almost expired." He illustrated the meaning of the word by what we would now call the artificial respiration of a person who has been nearly killed by drowning: "The flickering lamp of life in dying men suddenly flames up with unusual brightness."[14] He made it quite clear that revival can only be applied to a living soul, or to one that once lived. "To be revived is a blessing which can only be enjoyed by those who have some degree of life. Those who have no spiritual life are not, and cannot be, in the strictest sense of the term subjects of a revival."[15] He went on to say: "A true revival is to be looked for in the Church of God."[16] Spurgeon's books and pamphlets present us with his Biblical approach to revival; here we see his theological approach. Revival must begin with the church and with the church members; only then will it spread to the world outside. He continues this theological approach in the article by stating that revival "must result from the proclamation and receiving of

[13] *Op. cit.*, p. 529.
[14] *Ibid.*
[15] *Ibid.*
[16] *Ibid.*, p. 530.

living truth."[17] He disagreed strongly that revival can be worked up. He said that a revival is not the outcome of "excitement, crowded meetings, the stamping of the foot,"[18] it is the outcome of the proclamation of truth. "The Holy Ghost must come into the living heart through living truth."[19]

Finally he emphasized the seeking of revival by intercession in prayer meetings: "Let us pledge ourselves to form a prayer-union, a sacred band of suppliants, and may God do unto us according to our faith —

> 'Father for Thy promised blessing,
> Still we plead before Thy throne;
> For the time of sweet refreshing,
> Which can come from Thee alone.' "[20]

The article was written at the end of the same year in which practically the whole of the month of February had been given over at the Metropolitan Tabernacle for revival meetings. Early morning prayer meetings and communion services were held. Afternoon and evening meetings were held for Christian fellowship and prayer for revival. There were services in the afternoon and evening meetings for mission workers, tract distributors, lodging house evangelists, and so on.

The relationship which Spurgeon recognized between doctrine and revival he emphasized in *The Sword and the Trowel* in the year 1871:

> That great religious excitements have occurred apart from Gospel truth we admit; but anything which we, as believers in Christ, would call a genuine revival of religion, has always been attended with clear, evangelical instruction upon cardinal points of truth. What was the sinew and backbone of the Reformation? Was it not the clear enunciation of Gospel truths which the priesthood had withheld from the people? Justification by faith, starting like a giant from its sleep, called to its slumbering fellows; and together these great doctrines wrought marvels.

---

[17] *Ibid.*, p. 532.
[18] *Ibid.*
[19] *Ibid.*
[20] *Ibid.*

The Reformation was due not so much to the fact that Luther was earnest, Calvin learned, Zwingle brave, and Knox indefatigable, as to this — that the old truth was brought to the front, and to the poor the Gospel was preached. Had it not been for the doctrines which they taught, their zeal for holiness and their self-sacrifice, their ecclesiastical improvements would have been of no avail. The power lay not in Luther's hammer and nails, but in the truth of those theses which he fastened up in the sight of all men.[21]

As we have been before, he emphasized doctrine and prayer. He went on in his article:

When we read of Hugh Latimer on his knees perpetually crying, "O God, give back the Gospel to England," and sometimes praying so long that he could not rise, being an aged man, and they had to lift him up from the prison-floor, but he would still keep on crying, "O God, give back the Gospel to England," we may well wonder that some of us do not pray in the same way. The times are as bad as Latimer's, and we have as good need to pray as he had. . . . A revival is waiting, the cloud is hovering over England, and we do not know how to bring it down. Oh, that God may find some true spirits who shall be as conductors to bring down the fire Divine. We want it much, but our poor breathings — they do not come to much more — have no force, no expansiveness, no great heartedness, no prevalence in them.[22]

The same need for revival that year (1872) and his hopefulness that one would be sent from God, he expressed in these words: "There is a great need for a season of revival among the churches, and we have personal reason to believe that it is coming. If it be the Lord's will, a gracious time of refreshing will occur; and we think we have good warrant for anticipating it."[23]

Thus we are to think about revival, to anticipate it, to say on the authority of God's Word that if we fulfill the conditions laid down, we can anticipate that revival will come.

Later that year Spurgeon still expressed the same hope;

[21] *Op. cit.*, p. 216.
[22] *Ibid.*, 1872, p. 206.
[23] *Ibid.*, p. 1.

"O that the Lord would send forth real power into our midst! We need not great talents or intense excitements; with what we already have the battle may be won if the Lord will put His Spirit within us. The ox-goad, the jawbone, the sling-and-stone, and the ram's-horn trumpet, have each been made an irresistible weapon; with God the instrument is little, His might is everything. Only let us be strong in faith, full of zeal and very courageous for the Lord and our God, and the Lord will bless us."[24]

His own views as to the opposition that revivals created on the grounds of excitement, hysteria and so on, we can glean from an article in *The Sword and the Trowel* which he wrote in answer to a newspaper article in *The Times* in the year 1874. The editor, or the correspondent, writing in *The Times*, was criticizing an Anglican mission that was being attended by revival blessing. In the newspaper article there were some sweeping criticisms of revivals in general. It appears that the objection was first of all to the protracted length of the revival meetings, and so Spurgeon replied in this way: "Nobody has written to the papers to complain that daughters stayed out at an evening party after ten o'clock, or that his son came home a little before eleven from the opera. There is a good deal of cant in the irreligious world, and its hypocrisies are innumerable. That once in a while a meeting should be protracted beyond the hour allowed by prudence, is not so great a sin after all; it may be best to avoid it in every case, but should peculiar zeal and a special season of blessing lead a minister and a congregation into the error, we are not aware of any law, human or divine, which they will have violated."[25]

Answering the criticism of undue excitements by those attending the revival, Spurgeon wrote: "Men grow eager in the pursuit of wealth, and the pulse beats fast when great transactions are quivering in the balance; the world does

[24] *Ibid.*, p. 441.
[25] *The Sword and the Trowel*, 1874, p. 138.

not blame them for this, for it thinks the objects of their pursuit worthy of intense effort; but if a man grows earnest in seeking the salvation of his soul, he is censured for being too excited, and if he weeps for his sins, or rejoices when he has obtained pardon for them, he is set down at once, as being under the influence of fanatics and his confinement in Bedlam is confidently predicted. . . . Will any rational man maintain that excitement ceases to be legitimate according to the importance of the subject in hand? . . . Assuredly nothing in the nature of things, nothing in the realm of common sense, and certainly nothing in Holy Scripture can be urged against the legitimate use of excitement in religion. . . . The fact is that enthusiasm is only to be justified by the importance of its object."[26]

Nevertheless he concluded by deprecating the excesses of certain revivalists: "We lament the foolish rant and false doctrines which have poisoned former movements in certain quarters; but our solemn conviction is that the present gracious visitation which many parts of England and Scotland are enjoying is of the Lord, and should be hailed with delight by all gracious men. God speed it, we say, and make all the world to feel its power to the confusion of the hosts of evil and to the exaltation of the Son of God."[27]

There we see something of the breadth of the man's thought and his tolerance. He may have published a sermon on baptismal regeneration which set many of his Anglican friends against him, but when the Established Church has a mission which ends in revival he blesses them for it and says, "God speed it."

We can sum up all that Spurgeon wrote about revival by saying that here was a man who wrote about it frequently. By his pen he sought to make his own church, the men of his College, his magazine readers, long for revival and yearn over it. And when in the latter years of his ministry he did

[26] *Ibid.,* pp. 138, 139.
[27] *Ibid.,* p. 139.

not feel quite so confident and hopeful of a revival coming as he had earlier, we can explain it by the firm stand he had to take against lax doctrine, remembering his contention that doctrine and revival go together. As he saw false doctrine being preached, so he saw the hope of revival receding, and he spoke of the latter years of his ministry as "a heaviness in the air," "a hardening process going on," "when even curiosity seems dulled."[28] Such comments were not made in writing first of all, but in an address to ministers and students, later published under the title *An All-round Ministry*. This important volume will have to be considered with other post-1859 speeches and sermons.

[28] *Op. cit.*, pp. 304, 305.

WHAT SPURGEON SAID
ABOUT REVIVAL

IV

WHAT SPURGEON SAID ABOUT REVIVAL
Post-1859

SERMONS, SPEECHES AND ADDRESSES

If it is a Herculean task to read through 27 volumes of *The Sword and the Trowel* in order to discover what Spurgeon *wrote* about revival, what can we say of the research needed to cover 50 volumes of *The Metropolitan Tabernacle Pulpit* to find out what he *said* about spiritual awakenings? Many of these sermons contain important passages setting forth his views about revivals.

The index to these volumes of sermons lists only eleven specific addresses to do with revival, but Dr. C. T. Cook has rendered good service by collecting and editing twenty revival sermons for *The New Library of Spurgeon's Sermons* recently completed.*

There is a distinction between these sermons that are *about* revival, and the sermons which we shall be studying which were preached *during* revival. The revival-year sermons do not necessarily have to do with revival, but are addresses delivered during the revival year of 1859.

The index to the sermons indicates a line of study which is most fruitful. There are sermons in these volumes which deal with God's promise of revival, the prospect of revival, the means of bringing revival about, and so on.

First of all, before considering these sermons and ad-

* Published by Zondervan and Marshall, Morgan and Scott. Also known as the "Kelvedon Edition."

dresses which Spurgeon preached after the revival year of 1859, we must recall some earlier sermons preached before the revival in America had reached these shores, and before Spurgeon himself had even begun his own revival ministry in the Surrey Gardens Music Hall. While he was still preaching in the New Park Street Chapel in Southwark in November, 1856, Spurgeon took as his text Psalm 80:19, "Turn us again, O Lord God of hosts, cause thy face to shine; and we shall be saved." In that discourse he spoke of some of the beneficial effects of a spiritual awakening. He said that revival not only resulted in "the salvation of sinners" but in "the promotion of true love and unanimity" within the church. Also in the "stopping of the mouths of the enemies of truth"; and finally a revival promoted "the glory of God."[1] Such results were brought about by "revivals that we may consider to have been genuine . . . wrought by the instrumentality of such men as President Edwards in America and George Whitefield in this country, who preached a free-grace Gospel in all its fullness. Such revivals I consider to be genuine, and such revivals, I repeat again, would be a benefit to any church under Heaven."[2]

Referring to the revival which had begun in America in 1857 and spread to Great Britain two years later, he said when preaching in the Exeter Hall in the Strand: "Methinks I see the clouds floating hither; they have come from the far West, from the shore of America; they have crossed the sea, and the wind has wafted them till the green isle received the showers in its Northern extremity. Lo! the clouds are just now passing over Wales, and are refreshing the shires that border on the Principality. The rain is falling on Oxfordshire and Gloucestershire; divine grace is distilling, and the clouds are drawing nearer and nearer to us."[3]

This expectation was not unfounded. Spurgeon con-

[1] *Sermons on Revival*, Kelvedon Edition (New Library of Spurgeon's Sermons), pp. 56-58.
[2] *Ibid.*, p. 55.
[3] *Ibid.*, p. 143.

tinually expected revival blessing and it was not because of hearsay or second-hand information: "I have seen what I never saw before. It has been my lot these last six years to preach to crowded congregations, and to see many, many souls brought to Christ; it has been no unusual thing for us to see the greatest and the noblest of the land listening to the Word of God (this was obviously a reference to the three years' ministry in the Surrey Gardens Music Hall, when he saw the nobility sitting at his feet); but this week I have seen, I repeat, what mine eyes have never before beheld, used as I am to extraordinary things, I have seen the people of Dublin, without exception, from the highest to the lowest, crowd in to hear the Gospel. I have known that my congregation has been constituted in a considerable measure of Roman Catholics, and I have seen them listening to the Word with as much attention as if they had been Protestants."[4]

Turning to some particular and thrilling incidents, he told of his crossing by boat from Holyhead to Dublin. On both journeys to and from Ireland, the journey was exceptionally rough, but he spent the "most pleasant hours that I have ever spent."[5] All the sailors shook him by the hand and called him "Brother." One of them took out of his pocket a Welsh translation of Spurgeon's sermons with the preacher's photograph on the front cover and said that he read them every morning to his shipmates. On one occasion as this man was reading a sermon aloud and praying, a prospective passenger who was standing on the quay laughing and scoffing was suddenly smitten down, crying out for mercy, pleading with God for pardon. There were prayer meetings on the boat both before leaving England's shore and on arriving in Ireland. Although previously the sailors had been godless men, "yet by a sudden visitation of the Spirit of God they had all been converted."[6]

[4] *Ibid.*, p. 137.
[5] *Ibid.*, p. 138.
[6] *Ibid.*

Turning to his elders and deacons while he was preaching, Spurgeon declared: "There are grey-headed men around me who have known the Church of Christ sixty years, and I think they can bear me witness that they never knew such life, such vigour and activity, as there is at present."[7] It was not confined to Spurgeon's own church or even his denomination. He said: "The Church of England, Independents, Methodists and Baptists — there is not a single squadron that is behindhand; they have all their guns ready, and are standing, shoulder to shoulder, ready to make a tremendous charge against the common enemy. This leads me to hope, since I see the activity of God's ploughmen and vine dressers, that there is a great revival coming — that God will bless us, and that right early."[8] This spirit of expectation continued through Spurgeon's lifetime. He continued: "We read of such marvellous revivals one hundred years ago . . . now again God is about to send times of surprising fertility to His Church."[9]

In some of these post-1859 sermons on revival, Spurgeon described the pre-revival situation, that we have come to see is so characteristic of every period before a Holy Spirit awakening. In December, 1866, for instance, he said: "This is a wicked nation, this England; its wickedness belongs not to one class only but to all classes. Sin runs down our streets; we have a fringe of elegant morality, but behind it we have a mass of rottenness. There is not only the immorality of the streets at night, but look at the dishonesty of business men in high places. Cheating and thieving upon the grandest scale are winked at. Little thieves are punished, and great thieves are untouched. This is a wicked city, this city of London, and the land is full of drunkenness, and the land is full of fornication, and the land is full of theft, and the land is full of all manner of Popish idolatry."[10] No

---

[7] Ibid., p. 136.
[8] Ibid., p. 137.
[9] Ibid., p. 134.
[10] Ibid., p. 16.

wonder he took as his text on that occasion: "O Lord, revive thy work in the midst of the years" (Habakkuk 3:2). Such pessimistic passages, however, were never delivered without some such optimistic statement as this: "His Church can never sink to so low an ebb that He cannot soon build her up again, nor in our own hearts can the work of grace ever decline so grievously that the same mighty power that once quickened cannot revive and restore us."[11]

The more Spurgeon looked at the state of the world with its gross spiritual darkness, immorality and lawlessness, the more he felt the need of the church to be revived. The degeneration of the world only emphasized for him the corresponding decline in the church:

"What if it be true that within the last twelve months the Church of the living God has scarcely made the slightest approach to advance? . . . Do you ask me for the proofs? I can prove it, alas! too surely. Our own body, the Baptist Denomination, is up on the whole, and all things considered, in as sound and healthy a state as any Christian community now existing . . . but do you know what will have been the increase during the twelve months of the entire denomination in England, Scotland and Ireland, so far as we can ascertain it? . . . there will be no increase worthy of the name. In many parts of Wales, where we are strongest, there will be a positive decrease; and I think, in fifteen counties of England, we shall have lost members instead of making any advance."[12]

Preaching again from Habakkuk 3:2 and subsequently entitling the sermon, "A Message from God to His Church," he said that the prophet's prayer "is for a present and immediate revival of genuine religion,"[13] and he made Habakkuk's prayer his own.

Two years afterward in 1868 he said: "A revival is a

[11] *Metropolitan Tabernacle Pulpit*, No. 3514, "A Prospect of Revival," June, 1916, p. 253.
[12] *Sermons on Revival*, Kelvedon Edition, pp. 10, 11.
[13] *Ibid.*, p. 15.

great refreshing to the Church. I pray that a mighty wave may sweep over Great Britain, for much we need it."[14] "The great necessity of the Church," he declared, was "her being moved vigorously by the power of the Holy Spirit."[15]

Nevertheless in spite of this anticipation of coming revival, Spurgeon did not think that the church should be inactive and just sit and wait for the blessing, Micawber-fashion, waiting for something to turn up. He said the church's task was to pray for revival. Provided the longing was there, created in the heart by preaching and the Holy Spirit's influences, the church must "use every possible and right means to bring a revival."[16] The first means at the church's disposal was prayer, so long as her motives were right. The desire must not be for full churches, frequent conversions, flourishing organizations, but "God's glory that we want to see promoted."[17] "If this be the case may we not come very boldly?"[18]

The lack of spiritual prosperity and progress in the churches of our day and generation should cause us much heart-searching, making us ask with Spurgeon: "How much of this lies at my door? How much of this burden of God ought I to bear today? Certainly enough to lead us to such prayer as that before us (i.e. Habakkuk's prayer for revival)."[19]

Taking a text from the Prophet Ezekiel in July 1876 Spurgeon affirmed once more that prayer was the secret to revival blessing: "Christian men should never speak of 'getting up a revival.' Where are you going to get it up from? I do not know any place from which you can get it *up* except the place which it is better to have no connection with. We must bring revival down, if it is to be worth having. We must enquire of the Lord to do it for us. Too often the

[14] *Ibid.*, p. 105.
[15] *Ibid.*, p. 200.
[16] *Ibid.*, p. 47.
[17] *Ibid.*, p. 26.
[18] *Ibid.*
[19] *Ibid.*, p. 12.

temptation is to enquire for an eminent revivalist, or ask whether a great preacher could be induced to come. Now, I do not object to inviting soul-winning preachers, or to any other plans of usefulness; but our main business is to enquire of the Lord, for after all, He alone can give the increase."[20]

For those who were not used to attending prayer meetings, or who had forsaken this way to blessing, putting their trust in man-made methods, he declared: "Why has the Lord thus made prayer the necessary prelude to blessing? He has done so in great mercy to our souls. The Lord knows how beneficial it is to us to be much in prayer, and therefore He makes it easy for us to draw near to Him."[21]

Spurgeon's faith in the power of prayer to promote revival is never more firmly stated, and never more enthusiastically and infectiously, than in a message from Zephaniah 3:16-18, preached in October, 1887, the year of the Down Grade controversy when he made his protest against lax doctrine. Entitled "A Message for the Time Present," the sermon contained these words: "Oh, that we may see a great revival of religion. This is what we want before all things. This would smite the enemy upon the cheek-bone, and break the teeth of the adversary. If tens of thousands of souls were immediately saved by the sovereign grace of God, what a rebuke it would be to those who deny the faith! Oh, for times such as our fathers saw when Whitefield and his helpers began to preach the life-giving word! When one sweet voice was heard clear and loud, all the birds of paradise began to sing in concert with him, and the morning of a glorious day was heralded. If we are importunate in prayer, it must happen."[22]

In Exeter Hall, in 1860, he had already said: "Brethren, I sometimes hear of men called Revivalists, and I suppose it is imagined that there is some power in them or about

[20] *Ibid.*, p. 39.
[21] *Ibid.*, pp. 32, 33.
[22] *Ibid.*, p. 200.

them to create a revival. I should be sorry to wear the title lest I should be thought to arrogate any power to myself. I know, too, the people sometimes plan to have a revival at a certain time. As if the Spirit of God were at their disposal; as if they could make the wind, which bloweth where it listeth, and when it pleaseth, to come at their beck and at their command. I think all that is beginning at the wrong end. *Instead thereof we ought to hold meetings for prayer.*"[23]

His hearers then were urged time and again to pray for revival and not to be afraid of the accompanying enthusiasm. "If you read the story of the Reformation, or the later story of the new Reformation under Whitefield and Wesley, you are struck with the singular spirit that went with the preachers. The world said they were mad; the caricaturists drew them as being fanatical beyond all endurance; but there it was, their zeal was their power. Of course the world scoffed at that of which it was afraid. The world fears enthusiasm, the sacred enthusiasm which love to Christ kindles, the enthusiasm which is kindled by the thought of the ruin of men and by the desire to pluck the firebrands from the flame, the enthusiasm which believes in the Holy Ghost, which believes that God is still present with His Church to do wonders."[24]

Spurgeon's belief was that ultimately revival was all of God's sovereignty and of His Holy Spirit. In 1875 speaking from Isaiah 41:1, he said, "It is God the Omnipotent, who can make His Church mighty if He will, and that at once."[25] "God is absolute monarch of the hearts of men,"[26] he stated in a sermon entitled "A Revival Harvest" delivered in January, 1860. In the same address he said, "Divine Omnipotence is the doctrine of a revival."[27]

[23] *New Park Street Pulpit*, 1861, p. 475.
[24] *Sermons on Revival*, Kelvedon Edition, p. 15.
[25] *Ibid.*, p. 22.
[26] *Ibid.*, p. 133.
[27] *Ibid.*, p. 141.

WHAT SPURGEON SAID ABOUT REVIVAL

Of the power of the Holy Spirit he said, "What cannot the Spirit of God do? He sent tongues of fire at Pentecost ... and men of every nation heard the Gospel at once. He turned three thousand hearts by one sermon to know the crucified Saviour to be the Messiah. He sent the apostles like flames of fire through the whole earth, till every nation felt their power. He can do the like again. He can bring the Church out of darkness into noonday."[28]

In his preaching, as in his writing, Spurgeon's main emphasis was on right doctrine. He wanted a return to the doctrines proclaimed by John Bunyan and George Whitefield, "the doctrine of a reconciled God, to tell men that the Lord has laid help upon Jesus by punishing Him instead of us; to proclaim that there is life for a look at the crucified One, to tell them that the Holy Ghost creates men new creatures in Christ Jesus, to give a full and comprehensive view of the doctrines of grace; this is one of the surest ways under God of promoting a revival in religion."[29] He was more specific about the doctrines in "A Prospect of Revival." "Those grand doctrines of grace revealed to us in covenant, such as election, particular redemption, effectual calling, final perseverance, and the faithfulness of God."[30] These are the truths "which God usually blesses,"[31] and they of course were the doctrines which he preached during 1859 in the Surrey Gardens Music Hall. He was perfectly aware in 1876 of the general theological trend, and he said, "I could not conceive a Bunyan or a Baxter, or any other great soul-winner falling into these new notions, or if he did, there would be an end to his success."[32] Even in 1888, after he had made his Down Grade protest, and having seen something of the departure from sound doctrine in the pulpits of the land, he was not without hope and believed that even

[28] *Ibid.*, pp. 22, 23.
[29] *Ibid.*, p. 15.
[30] *Metropolitan Tabernacle Pulpit*, No. 3514, p. 256.
[31] *Sermons on Revival*, Kelvedon Edition, p. 78.
[32] *Ibid.*, p. 79.

if the church should say that she had finished with the very doctrines which he himself felt called to preach, and which he affirmed were revival-promoting doctrines, then "the truth will rise again. The eternal Gospel will burst her sepulchre. 'Vain the watch, the stone, the seal.' "[33]

Today Spurgeon's prophetic words are literally coming true. There is a revival of these very doctrines which he so powerfully proclaimed. Some people contemptuously call it "The new Puritanism," but even that is an indication that these old doctrines which Spurgeon proclaimed with such power and such effect are coming to the forefront again in many pulpits and printed religious works.

All the while that he was urging his hearers to pray for revival, and the preachers in his congregation to give their audiences sound doctrine when they returned to their pulpits, Spurgeon was experiencing the very blessing he was describing.

In 1874 he said in a sermon, "A Revival Promise": "We have enjoyed for many years a continuous visitation of grace. That which would be a revival anywhere else has been our ordinary condition, for which we are thankful. By the space of these twenty years, almost without rise or fall, God has continued to increase our numbers with souls saved by the preaching of His truth."[34] Spurgeon was not easily contented, however, and desired more and more blessing. "When will a greater blessing come? How can we obtain it? When shall we make some impression upon the mass of ungodly?"[35]

That Spurgeon knew the value of revival to a church we have already seen. He also knew the value of a revival convert to the church, as many other people have discovered before him and since. The man who is awakened during a revival is usually a bright and shining light on fire for God. It does not matter what upbringing he has had before

[33] Ibid., p. 255.
[34] Ibid., p. 82.
[35] Ibid., p. 81.

the revival affected him. He may not have been brought up in a Christian home. He may never have been trained in any religious influence such as the Sunday school, but such a man is usually superior to any other converted man. A person converted during revival days is usually quicker to grasp the truths of the Bible; he is a man who comes in a matter of days to a degree of spiritual maturity that may have taken ordinary converts many years to reach.

One of the most neglected aspects of the beneficial effects arising from a revival is the connection between revival and hymnology. Even in Dr. J. Edwin Orr's book, *The Second Evangelical Awakening in Great Britain*, there appears only a minor chapter at the end of the book about this subject. But Spurgeon pointed out that all true revivals of religion have been attended by a revival of song: "The joy that makes the heart grateful, enlivens the spirits, and diffuses happiness, will seek and must find some tuneful strains. Not to speak of the Hebrew Psalter or of the Greek Hymnals, in Luther's day his translation of the Psalms and his chorales did more to make the Reformation popular than even his preaching; for the ploughman at his field labour, and the housewife at the cradle would sing one of Luther's Psalms; so, too, in our own country in Wycliffe's day, fresh psalms and hymns were scattered all over the land. As you know how, in the last century, Wesley and Whitefield gave a new impetus to congregational singing. The hymns were printed in little flysheets after each sermon, and at length these units swelled into a volume. Collections and selections of hymns were published. So fond, indeed, were the Methodists of singing, that it became a taunt and a byword to speak of them as canting Psalm-singers. But this is the mark of a revived Church everywhere."[36]

Another much-neglected aspect of revival is that of the influence of a spiritual awakening upon children. Dr. Wilbur M. Smith writing in *Moody Monthly* (August,

[36] *Metropolitan Tabernacle Pulpit*, No. 3514, p. 261.

1959), stated that he had discovered that Spurgeon had much to say about revival and children. Dr. Smith recalled "a rich little volume" by Andrew Murray called *The Children for Christ*, in which there is a chapter based on Isaiah 44:3-5, entitled "God's Spirit in Our Children." Spurgeon preaching from this passage of Scripture said, "These conversions will come from all quarters. . . . Here is one who is the son of a deacon — we expected him to give his heart to Jesus. There is another, he is not a child of a religious professor but comes right out from an ungodly family. Ah, here is another, he has grown up and come to ripe years, having followed after folly and confirmed himself in sin, yet he comes forward, for the grace of God has called him. One comes from the wealthy, another comes from the poor, a third comes from nobody knows where; but they will and must come, for God knows His own and will call them. They shall come from all trades and occupations, from all Churches and denominations, from these little boys below me, I hope (boys from his Stockwell Orphanage)."[37]

Twenty years later he returned, as he often did, to the text upon which he had preached previously, and said: "If I were to promise for an unborn child that it should have red hair and a Roman nose, I should be quite as reasonable as if I promised that any child should become a child of God. I cannot do it; it is not within my power, nor within the power of any man. In any act of religion you yourself must be concerned. The godliest mother can pray for you, but you will not be saved unless you pray for yourself. The most believing father may use his faith on your behalf, but you will not be saved unless you yourself believe."[38]

Obviously a man like Spurgeon, who preached on at least four other occasions during the week besides twice on Sunday and on Thursday nights in his own church, must have spoken a great number of sermons and addresses

---

[37] *Moody Monthly*, 19 August 1959. Quotation by Dr. Wilbur M. Smith on p. 23.
[38] *Ibid.*, 1874, p. 20. *Note:* Kelvedon Edition edited at this point.

which were not published in the weekly issue of *The Metropolitan Tabernacle Pulpit*. We know that he addressed meetings as various as business men in Bishopsgate, students in his own college and Bristol Baptist College, the ministers of the London Baptist Association, and so on; besides which he spoke extemporaneously every Monday evening at the Tabernacle prayer meeting. He also delivered fund-raising lectures, such as "The History of Southwark" and "The Two Wesleys." In many of these speeches and addresses there were references to revival.

In his lecture on "The Two Wesleys," for instance (delivered at the Tabernacle in 1861), Spurgeon told his audience: "We have had some little specimens of revival through our land, but we have not had great and glorious shakings like those of that good time" (i.e. Wesley and Whitefield's day).[39] One of these minor specimens of revival which Spurgeon himself witnessed was in Wales. Spurgeon had gone to Wales for a rest, so he hoped, but was taken to a Welsh Chapel, and there "preached sermon after sermon until midnight."[40] He felt justified in keeping his congregation up as late as that, for he said as a result of those sermons there was "the conversion of a large number of men who afterwards lost their lives in the Risca Colliery explosion."[41]

Of the physical manifestations of revival, the excitement and the excesses attendant upon so many awakenings, he had something to say in an address to the students of his College. He said: "I had sooner risk the dangers of a tornado of religious excitement than see the air grow stagnant with a dead formality."[42]

To his own Tabernacle prayer meeting he said: "I am glad of any signs of life, even if they should be feverish and transient, and I am slow to judge any well-intended

[39] *Op. cit.*, p. 63.
[40] *Speeches at Home and Abroad*, p. 112.
[41] *Ibid.*
[42] *An All-round Ministry*, p. 181.

movement; but yet I am very fearful that many so-called 'revivals' have in the long run wrought more harm than good. Places which have had the most of religious excitement are frequently the most hard to reach. Men's minds have been baked hard in the oven of fanaticism. A species of religious gambling has fascinated many men, and given them a distaste for the sober business of true godliness. But if I would nail down counterfeits upon the counter, I do not therefore undervalue true gold. Far from it. It is to be desired beyond measure that the Lord would send a real and lasting revival of spiritual life."[43] In the same address he again stressed the need of prayer for revival: "It is suggested to me that we pray for a true and genuine revival of religion throughout the world."[44]

Spurgeon soon discovered what others had found out in America, that conversions took place in revival prayer meetings as well as in the ordinary services: "Dear friends, at our prayer meetings of late our Lord has graciously spoken to one and another of the unconverted among us."[45] He went on to say that it was God continuing the apostolic pattern of the *Acts*, for Pentecost "began with 'only a prayer meeting,' but ended with a great baptism of thousands of converts."[46] Requesting prayer for converts in the prayer meeting that night Spurgeon said: "By their conversion prove that a true revival has commenced tonight! Let it spread through all our households, and then run from Church to Church till the whole of Christendom shall be ablaze with the heaven-descended fire."[47]

The emphasis in all these speeches and sermons was again upon the need for sound doctrine allied to the prayers of God's people: "We want a revival of old-fashioned

---

[43] *The Sword and the Trowel*, 1885, p. 514.
[44] *Ibid.*
[45] *Ibid.*, p. 518.
[46] *Ibid.*
[47] *Ibid.*

Gospel preaching like that of Whitefield and Wesley; to me, preferably that of Whitefield."[48]

Holiness of life of the church member, was also a contributory factor toward the coming of revival upon the church as a whole. "Urgently do we need a revival of personal godliness," Spurgeon once said to his prayer meeting. "Brethren, we must each one live if the Church is to be alive; we must live unto God if we expect to see the pleasure of the Lord prospering in our hands. Sanctified men are the necessity of every age."[49]

Finally Spurgeon stressed the sovereignty of God in revival, in an evening sermon which was later published in his book, *Types and Emblems*. He had been preparing this sermon during a thunderstorm and cloudburst. He took as his text Ecclesiastes 11:3, "If the clouds be full of rain, they empty themselves upon the earth," and said: "This seemed to me like an example and an illustration of the sovereignty of God's dispensations. True is it in the spiritual as well as in the natural economy, that one place is rained upon, and another is not rained upon. In one part of the Church God's grace descends in a flood, while another part remains as dry and arid as the wilderness itself."[50]

There lies the mystery. In spite of all our praying, preaching and our personal holiness, the coming of revival is ultimately dependent upon the sovereign will of God, so that when it comes all we can say is:

"To God be the Glory,
Great things He hath done."

[48] *Ibid.*, pp. 514, 515.
[49] *Ibid.*, p. 515.
[50] *Op. cit.*, p. 217.

*WHAT SPURGEON PREACHED
DURING THE REVIVAL YEAR*

V

WHAT SPURGEON PREACHED DURING THE REVIVAL YEAR

We now have to consider the content of Spurgeon's 1859 sermons delivered in the Surrey Gardens Music Hall. These addresses are contained in two volumes entitled *The New Park Street Pulpit* for the year 1859 and then carried over into the year 1860.

The first of these sermons was delivered on January 2, 1859, and the last on December 18 of that year. We have already seen something of the doctrines that Spurgeon thought were most likely to promote revival — Divine Election, Human Depravity, Particular Redemption, Effectual Calling and Final Perseverance. He believed that revival would be the outcome of the revival of the preaching of these Calvinistic doctrines. These five doctrines are sometimes referred to as "the five points of Calvinism."

John Calvin (born 1509) was a great man. He had great qualities indeed as a theological thinker. His was not speculative theology, for it has been said that "whither the Bible took him, thither he went: where Scriptural declarations failed him, there he stopped short."[1] Others of course have gone further and have "out-Calvined Calvin!"

Now Calvinism can be summed up in the phrase, "the Sovereignty of God in grace."[2] Calvin was "pre-eminently the theologian of the Holy Spirit . . . It was he who first re-

---
[1] Warfield, B. B., *Calvin as a Theologian*, p. 5.
[2] *Ibid.*, p. 8.

lated the whole experience of salvation specifically to the working of the Holy Spirit, worked it out into its details, and contemplated its several steps and stages in orderly progress as the product of the Holy Spirit's specific work in applying salvation to the soul. Thus he gave systematic and adequate expression to the whole doctrine of the Holy Spirit and made it the assured possession of the Church of God."[3]

We have already seen that Spurgeon placed great emphasis on the work of the Holy Spirit in conversion. He once said, "We believe, in the first place, that God the Father elects His people; from before all worlds He chooses them to Himself; but let me ask you — what effect has the doctrine of election upon any man, until the Holy Spirit of God enters into Him? How do I know whether God has chosen me from before the foundation of the world? How can I possibly know? Can I climb to heaven and read the roll? . . . Election is a dead letter both in my consciousness and in any effect which it can produce upon me, until the Spirit of God calls me out of darkness into marvellous light. . . . It is a precious thing — that doctrine of election — to a child of God. But what makes it precious? Nothing but the influence of the Spirit. Until the Spirit opens the eye to read, until the Spirit imparts the mystic secret, no heart can know its election. No angel ever revealed to any man that he was chosen of God, but the Spirit of God doeth it."[4]

Calvin's emphasis was upon the supernatural in salvation. "The central fact of Calvinism is the vision of God. Its determining principle is a zeal for the Divine honour."[5] In our own days of rationalism, naturalism and materialism in this twentieth century, how we need a return to this emphasis of the supernatural in religion. As Professor War-

[3] *Ibid.*, pp. 8 and 9.
[4] *New Park Street Pulpit*, 1859, p. 212.
[5] *Calvin as a Theologian*, p. 26.

field points out: "A supernatural Redeemer is not needed for a natural salvation. If we can, and do, save ourselves, it were grossly incongruous that God should come down from Heaven to save us, trailing clouds of glory with Him as He came."[6] This is the core of Calvinism — a deep sense of man's hopelessness and helplessness without God's free grace. That it was also Spurgeon's belief we need have no doubt. He frequently stated in the Music Hall that he was no Arminian — that is a person who believes in human responsibility for eternal salvation and the need for man to cooperate with God (Arminius, a Dutch divine of the sixteenth century). On January 2, 1859, preaching on Psalm 138:8, Spurgeon said: "If there be one stitch in the celestial garment of my righteousness, which I am to insert myself, then I am lost . . . my confidence must not be in what I can do, or in what I have resolved to do, but entirely in what the Lord will do."[7]

He not only held such views himself and preached them fearlessly, but he had little patience with those who held them and yet feared to preach them. "Many of our Calvinistic preachers do not feed God's people. They believe in election, but they do not preach it. They think particular redemption true, but they lock it up in the chest of their creed, and never bring it out in their ministry. They hold final perseverance, but they persevere in keeping quiet about it. They think there is such a thing as effectual calling, but they do not think they are called effectually to preach it. The great fault we find with many is that they do not speak right out what they do believe."[8]

Many ministers, of course, holding Calvinistic views, have felt hampered by them from giving an open invitation to their sinful hearers to close with Christ and commit their lives to Him. Spurgeon felt so restricted in his early days of ministry, but he had surmounted this difficulty by 1859,

[6] *Ibid.*, p. 30.
[7] *New Park Street Pulpit*, 1859, p. 51.
[8] *Ibid.*, p. 151.

saying in October of that year: "There was a time, I must confess, when I somewhat faltered when about to give a free invitation. My doctrinal sentiments did at that time somewhat hamper me. I boldly avow that I am unchanged as to the doctrines I have preached; I preach Calvinism as high, as stern, and as sound as ever; but I do feel, and always did feel, an anxiety to invite sinners to Christ. And I do feel also, that not only is such a course consistent with the soundest doctrine; but that the other course is after all the unsound one, and has no title whatever to plead Scripture on its behalf."[9]

At the close of that year of revival, and in the last sermon to be preached in the Music Hall (December 11, 1859), Spurgeon summed up his Calvinistic ministry there by preaching on Acts 20:26, 27, noting that the apostle Paul had given his hearers the entire Gospel, not dwelling upon some one doctrine to the exclusion of the rest. Spurgeon said: "I question whether we have preached the whole counsel of God, unless predestination with all its solemnity and sureness be continually declared — unless election be boldly and nakedly taught as being one of the truths revealed of God. It is the minister's duty, beginning from this fountain-head, to trace all the other streams; dwelling on effectual calling, maintaining justification by faith, insisting upon the certain perseverance of the believer, and delighting to proclaim that gracious covenant in which all these things are contained, and which is sure to all the chosen blood-bought seed. . . . We are told that the times have changed: that we are to modify these old (so-called) Calvinistic doctrines, and bring them down to the tone of the times; that, in fact, they need dilution; that men have become so intelligent that we must pare off the angles of our religion, and make the square into a circle by rounding off the most prominent edges."[10] This he himself would not,

[9] *Ibid.*, p. 436.
[10] *Ibid.*, 1860, p. 26.

and did not do, either during 1859 in the Music Hall or subsequently during his thirty-one years' ministry at the Metropolitan Tabernacle.

A. Divine Election

Stated briefly, the doctrine of election is the belief in "Divine control of the steps leading up to acceptance of Christ."[11] In one sense election is the result of a previous predestination, that is, during the past ages of eternity, before the creation of the world and prior to human history, the triune Godhead determined and designed a plan of redemption in which fallen mankind would be raised to a higher position than that which Adam had attained before he fell into sin. Such a spiritual state was predestined by God, and that is "the wider issue," whereas election is predestination "carried into effect in time."[12] For our purposes, and for most preachers, Spurgeon included, the two words (election and predestination) come to mean practically the same thing and are almost interchangeable.

Let us consider first that covenant between the Trinity in heaven before the foundation of the world. Perhaps the finest passage that can be read in any of Spurgeon's sermons is one from an early sermon in the Music Hall in the revival year, when he has described with that vivid imagination of his, the Father, Son and the Holy Spirit planning salvation for sinful mankind:

> On the Father's part, thus runs the covenant. I cannot tell you it in the glorious celestial tongue in which it was written. I am fain to bring it down to the speech which suiteth to the ear of flesh, and to the heart of a mortal. Thus, I say, ran the covenant, in lines like these: "I, the Most High Jehovah, do hereby give unto my only begotten and well-beloved Son, a people countless beyond the number of the stars who shall be by Him washed from sin, by Him preserved, and kept, and led, and by Him, at last, presented before my throne, without spot, or wrinkle, or any such thing. I covenant by oath, and sware by

[11] Hammond, T. C., *In Understanding Be Men*, p. 111.
[12] *Ibid.*

myself, because I can sware by no greater, that those whom I now give to Christ shall be forever the objects of my eternal love. Them will I forgive through the merit of the blood. To these will I give a perfect righteousness; these will I adopt and make my sons and daughters, and these shall reign with me through Christ eternally." Thus ran that glorious side of the covenant.

The Holy Spirit also, as one of the high contracting parties on this side of the covenant, gave His declaration: "I hereby covenant," saith He, "that all whom the Father giveth to the Son, I will in due time quicken. I will show them their need of redemption; I will cut off from them all groundless hope, and destroy their refuges of lies. I will bring them to the blood of sprinkling; I will give them faith whereby this blood can be applied to them; I will work in them every grace; I will keep their faith alive; I will cleanse them and drive out all depravity from them, and they shall be presented at last spotless and faultless." This was the one side of the covenant, which is at this very day being fulfilled and scrupulously kept.

As for the other side of the covenant, this was the part of it, engaged and covenanted by Christ. He thus declared, and covenanted with His Father: "My Father, on my part I covenant that in the fullness of time I will become man. I will take upon myself the form and nature of the fallen race. I will live in their wretched world, and for my people will I keep the law perfectly. I will work out a spotless righteousness, which shall be acceptable to the demands of Thy just and holy law. In due time I will bear the sins of all my people. Thou shalt exact their debts on me; the chastisement of their peace will I endure, and by my stripes they shall be healed. My Father, I covenant and promise that I will be obedient unto death, even the death of the Cross. I will magnify Thy law, and make it honourable. I will suffer all they ought to have suffered. I will endure the curse of Thy law, and all the vials of Thy wrath shall be emptied and spent upon my head. I will then rise again; I will ascend into Heaven; I will intercede for them at Thy right hand; I will make myself responsible for every one of them, that not one of those whom Thou hast given me shall ever be lost, and I will bring all my sheep of whom, by Thy blood, Thou hast constituted me the shepherd — I will bring every one safe to Thee at last."

Thus ran the covenant and now, I think, you have a clear idea of what it was, and how it stands — the covenant between

God and Christ, between God the Father and God the Spirit, and God the Son as the covenant head and representative of all God's elect.[13]

We must go back from this important digression on the covenant to our study of the doctrine of election. The word "elect" is used but three times in the Old Testament — in Isaiah 42:1; 45:4; and 65:9 and 22. But its related words like "chosen" are used considerably more. In the New Testament "elect" is used quite a number of times, especially in the epistles (for example, Romans 9:11, I Thessalonians 1:4 and I Peter 1:10). In all these places it denotes "an act of Divine selection taking effect upon human objects so as to bring them into special and saving relationship with God."[14]

It is, of course, the elected community that has such an important position in the Old Testament. The children of Israel were the chosen people of God; privileged to be the race through whom God worked and revealed Himself and His ways to the world. An elect people were thus a race placed in a special position of favor and privilege. In the New Testament the emphasis is upon the individual. Corresponding with the Israel of the Old Testament we have the new Israel, the church of the New Testament; and the church is made up of individuals whom God has predestined and elected by sovereign grace.

Naturally this subject is fraught with mystery and with difficulty. We have finite minds. How can we begin to understand the inscrutable counsels of God? Now we only "know in part"; one day we shall know in full. How can we reconcile verses which teach that God's love embraces the world, that "whosoever will may come"; with the many texts and illustrations of God's love having a particular, favored object? Also, why does the Bible lay more stress on the fact that the saved have been predestined to salvation, while on the other hand, it is more reticent about the

[13] *New Park Street Pulpit*, 1859, pp. 419 and 420.
[14] *International Standard Bible Encyclopaedia*, Vol. 2, p. 925.

fact that the lost are predestined to eternal punishment? Are we chosen because of our capacity to believe, or do we believe because we have already been chosen? These are some of the kinds of difficulties that Spurgeon resolved for himself and for his hearers, at the same time giving them a vision of the sovereignty of God and the true meaning of God's grace. He turned their eyes away from the fault that is so common among us today — that of being surprised, or even angry that there should be anyone lost, to the greater surprise that any of us are deserving of being saved. Spurgeon's whole emphasis was upon our utter unworthiness and undeservedness, but God's free grace electing us to salvation.

One of the chief difficulties of the doctrine of election for many people is that they think it leads to sinful loose living. On the contrary, the doctrine truly held, fosters in the mind of the elect a desire to live a holy life rather than an unholy one. Spurgeon knew such people in his day. He said to his Music Hall congregation in January, 1859, that some of them were being told by Satan: "Thou art one of God's elect, and thou mayest live in sin, and do whatever thou pleasest." Then he added: "Such characters I hope are getting rare."[15]

This was, of course, the same difficulty that faced the apostle Paul. He had to write in Romans 6:1 and 2, "Shall we continue in sin, that grace may abound? God forbid. How shall we, that are dead to sin, live any longer therein?"

Perhaps the greatest difficulty for many people is concerning the non-elect. For Spurgeon the solution was simple; he always put the onus on man and not on God, by frequently quoting in his sermons —

"None are excluded hence,
But those who do themselves exclude."[16]

[15] *New Park Street Pulpit*, 1859, p. 56.
[16] *Ibid.*, p. 439.

Most of these difficulties, however, in the eyes of Spurgeon, were created by our own illogical thinking. "We begin to suppose impossibilities," he said on January 16, 1859. "Suppose . . . a sinner should come to Christ without Christ coming to Him, he would be lost. Well, that is very clear, only it is supposing a thing that could not happen; and what is the good of that? Suppose a child of God should live in sin, and die in sin, would he be saved? The thing is impossible. If you suppose yourself into a difficulty, you must suppose yourself out of it. It is like the old supposition, 'Suppose the moon were cream cheese, what would become of us on a dark night?' Christ said, 'No man can come unto Me, except the Father which hath sent Me, draw him.' If a sinner comes, he is drawn, or he would not have come."[17]

The benefits of realizing one's election vastly outweighed these difficulties for Spurgeon. Does election really tend toward lax sinful living? Far from it; its tendency is toward a life of prayer and piety: "The result of the believer's confidence — it leads him to prayer. . . . He has chosen no man who lives and dies presumptuously, trusting that he is chosen when he has no evidence of it. Do you live without prayer? Ah! soul; election hath nought to do with thee. . . . A genuine confidence in God does not lead us to give up prayer, but leads us to prayer."[18] So our confidence in election leads us to holy living.

Spurgeon well knew why some disliked the doctrine of election and hated those who taught it. Preaching a sermon on Free Grace in the Music Hall on January 9, 1859, he drew a parallel between the non-election of fallen angels, allowed by God "to expiate their offences in the fires of hell,"[19] and the election of men. Everyone approves of the latter being elect and the former non-elected, and Calvinism is approved, until he realizes that some men are

[17] *Ibid.*, p. 79.
[18] *Ibid.*, pp. 56 and 57.
[19] *Ibid.*, p. 66.

saved and others are not. Pride has entered into the human heart at that point; mankind thinks himself so clever, so worthy of being elected, that to think that God should choose us on grounds other than our human merit is a severe blow to our pride. "The only reason why God selected the vessels of mercy must have been because He would do it. There was nothing in any one of them which caused God to choose them. We all were alike, all lost, all ruined by the fall; all without the slightest claim upon His mercy; all, in fact, deserving of His utmost vengeance."[20]

It can be seen why so many disliked Spurgeon's preaching. They thought that because of their advantages; their position, possessions, learning, decency and code of morals, that they ought to be one of those whom God was sure to have elected; but God does not choose on those grounds, for He sees us all as ruined, depraved and sinful.

Preaching on "Predestination and Calling" in March of the revival year, Spurgeon declared that "men hated election just as thieves hate Chubb's patent locks; because they cannot get at the treasure themselves, they therefore hate the guard which protects it. . . . These men will not repent, will not believe; they will not go God's way, and then they grumble and growl, and fret and fume, because God has locked the treasure up against them. Let a man once believe that all the treasure within is his, and then the stouter the bolt, and the surer the lock, the better for him. Oh, how sweet it is to believe our names were on Jehovah's heart and graven on Jesus' hands before the universe had a being."[21]

It can be clearly seen that Spurgeon's emphasis all the time is upon the sovereignty of God. Being what He is, omniscient; His will being immutable; His ways past finding out — election is therefore in keeping with His sovereignty; humanity dare not question it. As our Lord Jesus Christ

[20] *Ibid.*, p. 67.
[21] *Ibid.*, p. 135.

believed and spoke about it, we have no grounds for unbelief. "What said Christ? 'I pray for them: I pray not for the world, but for them which thou hast given me: for they are thine.' If Christ prayeth for none but for His chosen, why should ye be angry that ye are also taught from the Word of God that in the covenant there was provision made for the like person, that they might receive eternal life."[22]

Speaking of divine election as an infallible proof of divine compassion, God's great love for the sinner, Spurgeon used this illustration in Free Grace: "Now if her Majesty the Queen, having in her hands the sovereign power of life and death, chooses that this man shall not die, but that he shall be spared, do you not see as plain as daylight, that the only reason that can move her to spare that man, must be her own love, her own compassion? For, as I have already supposed, there is nothing in that man's character that can be a plea for mercy, but that, contrariwise, his whole character cries aloud for vengeance against his sin. Whether we like it or not, this is just the truth concerning ourselves."[23]

The question that Spurgeon was continually endeavoring to answer was the one that he knew he would be putting into his hearers' minds by preaching this doctrine. "How am I to know whether I am predestined by God unto eternal life or no? . . . Until this question be answered my heart cannot rest, for I am intensely anxious about it."[24] "Some men want to know whether they are elect. We cannot tell them unless they will tell us this. Dost thou believe? Is thy faith fixed on the precious blood? Then thou art in the covenant. . . . He that believeth is elected. . . . Thou canst not see thine election with the naked eye; but through the blood of Christ, thou canst see it clear enough. Trust thou in the blood, poor sinner, and then the blood of the

[22] *Ibid.*, p. 420.
[23] *Ibid.*, p. 69.
[24] *Ibid.*, p. 129.

everlasting covenant is proof that thou art an heir of heaven."[25] The emphasis is thus upon human cooperation with the divine control, faith being the mode. Or, as he expressed it in a sermon entitled "Holy Violence" (May, 1859): "'Oh!' says one, 'I thought it was all the work of God.' So it is, from first to last. But when God has begun the work in the soul, the constant effect of God's work in us is to set us working; and where God's Spirit is really striving with us, we shall begin to strive too."[26]

We have not, then, given a detailed description of the doctrine of election by C. H. Spurgeon, nor have we set out to define or to defend it adequately. We have not attempted a complete explanation of all the difficulties. For that we should have to turn to a consideration of the complete set of volumes of Spurgeon's published sermons, and the index to these volumes reveals that he dealt with practically every Scriptural reference to the doctrine of election, some of them several times during his long ministry at the Tabernacle. We have only been dealing with his presentation and his proclamation of this doctrine during the year of revival, 1859, and only these sermons which were preached to the hosts of unsaved in the Music Hall (not those addresses which were preached to his own church members in New Park Street Chapel). Remembering again that he preached to approximately 10,000 people each Sunday morning in the Music Hall, the majority actually unsaved, no one could ever charge Spurgeon with preaching an "easy-believism" gospel, such as so many of us are guilty of preaching today. It was not a mere call "to follow Christ," "to give your heart to Christ," "to come to the front and sign on the dotted line," "to fill in a decision card," "to come into the counselling room." There was none of this with Spurgeon. We have only to study once again the very effective passage where he describes the covenant

[25] *Ibid.*, pp. 424 and 425.
[26] *Ibid.*, p. 217.

made in the distant ages of past eternity to realize that here was a Gospel which resulted in solid conversions; there was none of the superficiality about the Christianity of his day that we know in our time.

We have not, of course, made a study of his public prayers in which he is alleged to have prayed more than once: "Oh God, save Thine elect, and then elect some more!" It is not true to say, however, that Spurgeon was a Calvinist on his knees and an Arminian on his feet, that he believed in election when he was praying but that he believed in a "whosoever-will Gospel" when he was preaching. He was a Calvinist whether on his knees or on his feet, in his praying and in his preaching. Simply because, as he said, the elect had not got a chalk mark on their backs to distinguish them from the rest of his congregation, he preached to them as if all were chosen and were to be saved. Only the effectual nature of the call or otherwise would decide; but what Spurgeon meant by effectual calling is a later consideration.

B. HUMAN DEPRAVITY

The doctrine of human depravity is sometimes known as "total depravity." The late Dr. P. W. Evans of Spurgeon's College used to illustrate this doctrine in a very simple way for his students. He used to say: "If you take a glass of water, and hold your fountain pen over it, and let one drop fall into the glass you have totally depraved the water." Or, he would say: "Instead of using a glass of water you could go to a lake, and still one tiny drop of ink dropped in the lake will have been sufficient to taint the whole."

Early in the life of small children can be perceived the signs of sin and moral weaknesses. They need no one to teach them; they readily fall into such sins as deceitfulness, untruthfulness, vindictiveness, and even stealing. A child needs no education in *doing* evil, but constant correction is needed by the parents if a child is to live a life that is morally good and decent.

Everyone, then, is born with a tendency to sin; as all wood has a grain, so everyone has a natural "pull" or tendency toward evil and wickedness. This is not only the concern of theologians; this is a problem which has confronted educators and philosophers down through the ages.

On the surface some men and women seem to live lives which the world describes as decent, noble, or heroic. Nevertheless, underneath the surface a close examination reveals that they are not untainted, and in any case the total record of evil in the world obviously vastly outweighs the total sum of good. And a man who is seemingly perfect according to the world's ideas is still imperfect according to God's standards. The Lord Jesus Christ had a conversation with a morally good man, or so he appeared, for he was a man who had kept the commandments from his youth up, but to him Jesus said, "One thing thou lackest." So everyone of us has either broken some commandment, or there has been a time in our life when we have harbored unbelief toward God and Jesus Christ. We have spent days when we have been apathetic and indifferent about spiritual things, and the Bible summarizes this condition by using such terms as alienation from God, spiritual deadness or death, blindness, or living in darkness. Theologians affirm that the root of the trouble is original sin.

Again, this is a greatly misunderstood doctrine, chiefly because of a change in meaning of the word "original." The Oxford Dictionary's first meaning of the word is "existent from the first, primitive," and the example given in parenthesis is original sin. This is then defined as "innate depravity common to all in consequence of the fall." But the second meaning of the word "original" is "novel in style or in character," "inventive." Thus when we speak of a child having original sin, in our mind's eye we tend to think of a child's inventiveness in producing new forms of wickedness, and some of them are highly apt at this!

But that is not the way original is meant by the theologians. Original sin for them is Adam's sin imputed to all his descendants, with its guilt. The Shorter Catechism puts it: "The sinfulness of that estate whereinto man fell, consists in, the guilt of Adam's first sin, the want of original righteousness, and the corruption of his whole nature, which is commonly called original sin; together with all actual transgressions which proceed from it." As Dr. J. Gresham Machen put it: "The Bible teaches . . . that every man comes into the world a sinner, with a corruption of nature out of which all individual transgressions proceed. That is the doctrine of original sin."[1] The sin which is in every one of us from the day of our birth is the actual sin of Adam, carrying with it the actual guilt of Adam, imparted to us, and this original sin of our first parents has pervaded our being in every part.

Now of course this belief in original sin which has depraved our moral and spiritual natures is not something which only Calvinists believe. Arminians also believe that mankind is sinful and alienated from God by their wickedness. Both Calvinists and Arminians adopt in their preaching the attitude that man must be told of his dire plight and be urged to have repentance toward God and faith in Jesus Christ.

It must be confessed that many preachers have done a great deal of harm by their presentation of this doctrine of human depravity, for they have given people the idea that total depravity means that men and women are mere depraved beasts; as if they indulged in the worst kinds of wickedness imaginable, and were utterly corrupt in all their ways. That is not the true meaning of the doctrine of human depravity. It is certainly not what our Puritan forefathers taught. It is in no sense what Spurgeon preached.

[1] *The Christian View of Man*, p. 272.

These men simply meant that sin has affected man *in toto*, in every part of his being, mind, soul and body; the principle of evil extends to the whole of his nature. The word "total" therefore governs the field in which sin is operative, that is, the whole of man's nature, and not the degree of sinfulness into which he has fallen.

T. C. Hammond uses an illustration as simple as that of Dr. Evans. He says: "A line that is not the shortest distance between two points is crooked or depraved (i.e., turned aside). If it cannot straighten itself, it is totally depraved, whether it is an inch or a mile out of plumb."[2]

That seems a satisfying illustration of total depravity; but perhaps now the simplest definition of this doctrine is by another American theologian, Dr. E. Y. Mullins: "In brief, it means that all the parts of our nature have been affected by sin."[3] Proceeding to amplify that simple definition he continues: "It does not mean that men are as bad as they can be, nor that all men are equally bad . . .it means rather that human nature, as such, and in all its parts in its unregenerate state, is under the dominion of sin."[4] There is Scriptural authority and confirmation of such definitions in Genesis 6:5 and 12; Psalm 14:2 and 3; Romans 8:7 and 8 etc.

With the advance of education in general and moral philosophy in particular, this doctrine has been "soft-pedalled" by preachers. Many Christian leaders have felt that this doctrine is most unpalatable in an age when mankind has become so clever. We have made so many discoveries and inventions that we have come to look upon human nature as inherently good. Then again, after a world war, when so many young men (and young women, too, in the second) have laid down their lives sacrificially for friends and for country, we dislike this doctrine that emphasizes man's badness. When men and women have been so "noble"

[2] *In Understanding Be Men*, p. 96.
[3] *The Christian Religion in Its Doctrinal Expression*, p. 294.
[4] *Ibid.*

as we call it, then we cannot reconcile this nobility with total depravity.

If revival is largely dependent upon correct doctrine, as Spurgeon contended, then we return to a positive and powerful declaration of human depravity, in spite of our twentieth century veneer of respectability and social conventionality. Before God we stand as totally depraved throughout our natures.

Spurgeon made his position quite clear even before the revival year of 1859. Preaching in Exeter Hall, the Strand, in April, 1855, he declared: "There is much to sadden us in a view of the ruins of our race. As the Carthaginian who might tread the desolate site of his much-loved city, would shed many tears when he saw it laid in heaps by the Romans; or as the Jew, wandering through the deserted streets of Jerusalem, would lament that the ploughshare had marred the beauty and the glory of that city which was the joy of the whole earth; so ought we to mourn for ourselves and our race, when we behold the ruins of that godly structure which God has piled, that creature, matchless in symmetry, second only to angelic intellect, that mighty being, man, — when we behold how he is 'fallen, fallen, fallen, from his high estate,' and lies in a mass of destruction."[5]

He went on in that sermon (his text was Romans 8:7) to describe how the depravity of man was total, although he preferred to use the word "universality" on that occasion. There was a universality in that "all persons," "all times" and "the whole of the mind"[6] were involved. Expanding that phrase, "the whole of the mind," Spurgeon said that the question was often asked: "What part of man was injured by the fall?" His answer was, "I believe that fall crushed man entirely . . . the whole of man is defaced."[7]

[5] *New Park Street Pulpit*, 1855, p. 149.
[6] *Ibid.*, pp. 152, 153.
[7] *Ibid.*, p. 153.

The whole of man for him included memory, affections, imagination, judgment and conscience.

Human depravity resulted in human inability, according to Spurgeon. Preaching a sermon by that title ("Human Inability," March 7, 1858), a year before the revival, he said: "Through the fall, and through our own sin, the nature of man has become so debased and depraved, and corrupt, that it is impossible for him to come to Christ without the assistance of God the Holy Spirit."[8]

During 1859, Spurgeon was just as definite in his proclamation of this doctrine of human depravity. He admitted, as we have already seen, that the doctrine does not declare that man cannot be good in certain aspects of daily living, and that an unregenerate man cannot do a great deal of good, and a great many kind acts to his fellowmen. What Spurgeon pointed out, however, was that this goodness was not in the sphere of spiritual things. Preaching on January 23, 1859, on the text: "O wretched man that I am! Who shall deliver me from the body of this death? I thank God through Jesus Christ our Lord" (Romans 7: 24, 25), Spurgeon said: "Carnal men, unrenewed men, have one nature — a nature which they inherited from their parents, and which, through the ancient transgression of Adam, is evil, only evil, and that continually (he begins by admitting original sin). Mere human nature, such as is common to every man, has in it many excellent traits, judging of it between man and man. A merely natural man may be honest, upright, kind and generous, he may have noble and generous thoughts, and may attain unto a true and manly speech; but when we come to matters of religion, spiritual matters that concern God and eternity, the natural man can do nothing. The carnal mind, whosesoever mind it may be, is fallen, and is at enmity to God, does not know the things of God, nor can it ever know them. Now when

[8] *Ibid.*, 1858, p. 138.

a man becomes a Christian, he becomes so through the infusion of a new nature."[9]

Spurgeon truly taught that depravity was total and universal during 1859: "Understand, then, that the old nature of the Christian is a body; it has in it a substance, or, as Calvin puts it, it is a *mass* of corruption. It is not simply a shred, a remnant — the clout of the old garment; but the whole of it is there still. True, it is crushed beneath the foot of grace; it is cast out of its throne; but it is there, there in all its entireness, and in all its sad tangibility, a body of death."[10]

For Spurgeon the universality of human depravity was such that it included the tiniest infant. On October 30, 1859, preaching on Revelation 19:12 — "On His head were many crowns," he imagined some of the redeemed in heaven. Included in their number were the glorious myriad of infants, who compose the family above. "We from our mother's breasts fled straight to Heaven, redeemed by the blood of Christ. We were washed from original depravity, and we have entered heaven."[11] These young children were too young to have sinned consciously or deliberately, not having reached the years of discretion or accountability; yet for Spurgeon they still had original sin within their hearts as the result of the fall of man, and God in His love and mercy provided the covering of the blood of Jesus Christ, that these infants might form part of the redeemed host of heaven.

During 1859, Spurgeon described man's depravity by using two Scriptural terms: death and disease. On May 8 he preached from Ezekiel 26:27 ("And I will put My Spirit within you") and said: "Remember what man is by nature. . . . Holy Scripture tells us that man by nature is *dead* in trespasses and sins. It does not say that he is sick, that he is faint, that he has grown callous, and hardened, and

[9] *Ibid.*, 1859, p. 82.
[10] *Ibid.*, p. 83.
[11] *Ibid.*, p. 455.

seared, but it says he is absolutely dead. Whatever that term 'death' means in connection with the body, that it means in connection with man's soul, viewing it in its relation to spiritual things. When the body is dead it is powerless; it is unable to do anything for itself; and when the soul of man is dead, in a spiritual sense, it must be, if there is any meaning in the figure, utterly and entirely powerless, and unable to do anything of itself or for itself. . . . The drift of the Gospel is, that man is dead in sin, and that Divine life is God's gift. But Scripture does not only tell us that man is dead in sin; it tells us something worse than this, namely, that he is utterly and entirely averse to anything that is good and right. . . . Turn you all Scripture through, and find continually the will of man described as being contrary to the things of God. . . . Here lies the deadly mischief; not only that he is powerless to do good, but that he is powerful enough to do that which is wrong, and that his will is desperately set against everything that is right. . . . Once get the correct view, that man is utterly fallen, powerless, guilty, defiled, lost, condemned, and you must be sound on all points of the great Gospel of Jesus Christ. Once believe man to be what the Scripture says he is — once believe his heart to be depraved, his affections perverted, his understanding darkened, his will perverse, and you must hold that if such a wretch as that be saved, it must be the work of the Spirit of God, and the Spirit of God alone."[12]

Human depravity, therefore, was the pivot point upon which the other four points of Calvinism swung for C. H. Spurgeon. Once accept the depravity of man's nature, then it was easy to accept election, redemption, calling, and the final perseverance of the saints.

Describing human depravity as a disease, Spurgeon based his message on Hosea 10:2, "Their heart is divided; now shall they be found faulty."[13] Spurgeon said that a divided heart was:

[12] *Ibid.*, p. 210.
[13] *Ibid.*, p. 409.

a fearful disease. It affects a vital part; it is not merely a disease of the hand, that reformation might cure; it is not merely a disease of the foot, that restraint might sometimes mollify; it is not merely a disease of the eye that which hath but to be couched to let the light stream in upon it. It is a disease of a vital region — of the heart, a disease in a part so vital that it affects the whole man. The utmost extremity of the frame suffers when once the heart becomes affected, and especially so affected as to be divided. There is no power, no passion, there is no motive, no principle, which does not become vitiated when once the heart is diseased. . . . The disease here described, not only deals with a vital part, but toucheth it after a most serious fashion. It doth not simply say the heart palpitates; it doth not declare that the life-floods that issue from it have become more shallow and less rapid, but it declares something worse than all these, namely, that the heart was cleft in twain, and utterly divided. A stony heart may be turned to flesh, but turn a divided heart into whatsoever you please, so long as it is divided, all is ill. . . . It is a division in itself peculiarly loathsome. . . . If a man had spots upon his countenance, or some disease that stared everyone else in the face, as often as he was beheld, surely he would retire from society and endeavour to keep himself a recluse. But not so the man with a divided heart. He goes everywhere, utterly unconscious that his disease is of the most loathsome character. . . . Not merely is the disease loathsome, but I must observe it is one always difficult to cure, because it is chronic. It is not an acute disease, which brings pain, and suffering, and sorrow with it, but it is chronic; it has got into the very nature of the man. . . . This is a disease which enters into the very nature, and will lie in the blood; though the most powerful medicines search it out. (This) disease is deeply rooted within . . . and if left alone it will come to a most dreadful end — its end is sure destruction.[14]

It can be seen that Spurgeon preached, with such vivid description and with sanctified imagination, to make sinful hearers aware of their depravity. He well knew that they would be self-satisfied, and worse still self-righteous, until they were awakened to their condition and their need. In February, 1859, preaching a sermon subsequently entitled "Reform," he said: "Until we are brought to know

[14] *Ibid.*, pp. 410, 411.

our own lost and ruined condition, self-righteousness is the god before which every one of us will prostrate ourselves. . . . Let us go home and prostrate ourselves before God and cry, 'Vile and full of sin I am.' "[15]

That human depravity and man's inability to save himself were truths which ran alongside one another for Spurgeon we have already seen in many of these extracts from the revival year sermons, but perhaps never more clearly than in an address called "Man's Ruin and God's Remedy" preached in November, 1859: "Sinner, there is this to aggravate to thy case and increase thine alarm — thy helplessness, thy utter inability to do anything to save thyself, even if God should offer thee the chance. . . . Thou sayest, 'I will repent.' Nay, thou canst not. Repentance is not possible to thee as thou art, unless God gives it to thee. . . . You cannot repent of yourself. . . . Recollect, sinner, thou art so lost, so ruined, so undone, that thou canst do nothing to save thyself. Thine inability is so great, that unless God pull thee up out of the pit into which thou hast fallen, thou must lie there and rot to all eternity. Thou art so undone that thou must lie there and rot to all eternity. Thou art so undone that thou canst neither stir hand, nor foot, nor lip, nor heart, unless grace help thee."[16]

The sinner's inability was always matched by the Saviour's ability and willingness for Spurgeon. In the same sermon he concluded: "You know I was to show that Christ could overcome our depravity. And He has done it in some of you while I have been speaking. Do not believe your heart when it says that Christ will shut you out and will not pardon you: come and try Him, come and try Him; and the first one that is shut out, I will agree to be shut out with him."[17]

Expecting some of his hearers thus to be converted while he was actually preaching, he sent the undecided

[15] *Ibid.*, p. 106.
[16] *Ibid.*, p. 484.
[17] *Ibid.*, p. 488.

home to think again, urging them to dwell deep on their depravity. "Not only is the world lost," he said, "but you are lost yourself; not only has sin defiled the race, but you yourself are stained by sin."[18]

According to Dr. J. Gresham Machen in his book, *The Christian View of Man*, total depravity is more than mankind being "totally corrupt," it is mankind "totally unable to please God."[19] Expanding that statement he adds: "the Biblical doctrine of total depravity means that nothing that fallen and unregenerate men can do is really well-pleasing to God. Many things they do are able to please us, with our imperfect standards, but nothing that they do is able to please God; nothing that they do can stand in the white light of His judgment-throne. Some of their actions may be relatively good, but none of them are really good. All of them are affected by the deep depravity of the fallen human nature from which they come."[20]

That side of human depravity also received Spurgeon's attention. "The acceptable acts of the Christian's life cannot be performed without the Spirit," he said in a sermon entitled "The Necessity of the Spirit's Work."[21] "Everything . . . that we do without the Spirit is unacceptable to God."[22]

In "A Divided Heart" Spurgeon tried to uncover some of the cloaks by which depraved men seek to curry favor with God, through formal religion, enthusiasm to do good, etc., and commented: "A pure and Holy God hates, first (a man's) sin, and secondly, the lies with which he endeavours to cover it. . . . God hates sin anywhere, but when sin puts its finger upon His Divine altar; when it comes and lays its insolent hand on the sacrifice that is burning there, then God spurns it from Him with disgust."[23]

Thus the eminent scientist was correct who declared

[18] *Ibid.*, p. 482.
[19] *Op. cit.*, p. 289.
[20] *Ibid.*, p. 290.
[21] *New Park Street Pulpit*, p. 215.
[22] *Ibid.*, p. 216.
[23] *Ibid.*, pp. 414, 415.

that "from the point of view of science, Calvinism is 'the only respectable theology.' Calvinism alone does justice to the unity of the world, as it certainly alone does justice to the teaching of the Bible."[24] Granted the sovereignty of God which is the very core of Calvinism, and the depravity of man, of which we have daily evidence in our newspapers, and also man's inability to save himself which human history attests, the logical outcome must be that man who is so hopelessly depraved and utterly helpless must be elected, predestined to salvation, and the Holy Spirit must call him with an effectual call. Since God is a sovereign God, then His particular redeemed ones must persevere right to the end.

C. Particular Redemption

We have already noted that in the year 1858, that is twelve months before the great revival year, Spurgeon explained in a sermon in the Surrey Gardens Music Hall how the pattern of his preaching was going to change. From that time on he said he was going to deal with the great truths which he believed lay at the very foundation or basis of the Christian religion. "The doctrine of redemption," he said, "is one of the most important doctrines of the system of faith. A mistake on this point will inevitably lead to a mistake through the entire system of our belief."[1] Particular Redemption for Spurgeon was the pivot point upon which swivelled Election and Depravity on the one side, and Calling and Final Perseverance on the other. Redemption was the central doctrine for him. He believed that he who went wrong on redemption went wrong on the rest. He went on to explain what the Arminians and the Calvinists believed about Christ's death, pointing out that the former believed that Christ died to make the salvation of all men possible and that salvation depended upon a man's will, his voluntary surrender to the Lord Jesus Christ. By contrast,

[24] *The Christian View of Man*, p. 46. Quoted by J. G. Machen.
[1] *New Park Street Pulpit*, 1858, p. 130.

however, the followers of Calvin, among whom he counted himself, said, "Now we believe in no such thing. We hold that Christ, when He died, had an object in view, and that object will most assuredly and beyond a doubt, be accomplished. We measure the design of Christ's death by the effect of it."[2] That object for Spurgeon was the salvation of God's elect. He believed that the Lord Jesus Christ died for "a multitude that no man could number, and . . . as a result of this, every person for whom He died must, beyond a shadow of doubt, be cleansed from sin, and stand, washed in blood, before the Father's throne."[3]

At first sight the doctrine of Particular Redemption seems little different from that of Divine Election. In fact, in 1857 Spurgeon preached a sermon which he entitled "Particular Election,"[4] not Particular Redemption. If election is God's sovereign choice of certain men and women to eternal salvation, are the elect therefore not the particular ones whom Christ died to redeem? Within that query we have a distinction that provides the answer to the question. Election is God at work; Particular Redemption is the Son working. Election is God's choice; Redemption is the Saviour's substitutionary death on the cross for those whom God, in His sovereignty, has chosen to be redeemed. Redemption then is carrying into effect the election. If Christ died as a substitute then a substitute represents a definite, particular person. Therefore He died as the substitute for each one of those particular people whom God in His wisdom and sovereignty had chosen.

Of course, the opponents of this doctrine which Spurgeon proclaimed so dogmatically and with such power found many texts to quote in opposition, for example John 3:16, "For God so loved the world that He gave His only begotten Son, that whosoever believeth in Him should not perish, but have everlasting life." They affirm that that is

[2] *Ibid.*
[3] *Ibid.*
[4] *Ibid.*, 1857, p. 129.

a text emphasizing the universal nature of Christ's redemption — it contains two words "whosoever" (which includes anyone), and "the world" (which includes everyone). Side by side with that they quote a verse like II Corinthians 5:14, "(Christ) died for all"; "He is the propitiation for our sins; and not for ours only, but also for the sins of the whole world" (I John 2:2). Now there are two different answers which can be given to such texts. The first is to quote other texts like: "To give His life a ransom for many" (Matthew 20:28). The other answer depends upon the meaning of words. "World" and "all" are used frequently in Scripture, but they do not have a literal meaning in every case. Spurgeon pointed out in a sermon on "Particular Redemption" in 1858: " 'The whole world is gone after Him.' Did all the world go after Christ? 'Then went all Judea, and were baptized of Him in Jordan.' Was all Judea or all Jerusalem baptized in Jordan? 'The whole world lieth in the wicked one.' Does the whole world there mean everybody? If so, how was it, then, that there were some who were 'of God'? The words 'world,' and 'all,' are used in some seven or eight senses in Scripture; and it is very rarely that 'all' means all persons, taken individually. The words are generally used to signify that Christ has redeemed some of all sorts — some Jews, some Gentiles, some rich, some poor, and has not restricted His redemption to either Jew or Gentile."[5]

The critics of Calvinism also speak about "a limited atonement." They say that those who preach this doctrine which Spurgeon preached of Particular Redemption are preaching a limited atonement; that they are preaching that the Lord Jesus Christ's atonement for sinners was limited to a few. It is the critic who uses the word few, not the Calvinist. The Calvinist believes that the Lord Jesus Christ died for a particular people, he does not say for a particular *few*. He believes the text quoted by Spurgeon that Christ "gave His life as a ransom for many," and that one day in

[5] *Ibid.*, 1858, p. 136.

heaven there will be a "multitude which no man can number." C. H. Spurgeon was careful to point out that far from limiting God by this doctrine, God is only limited by human sin. Sin has enslaved men and in their sinfulness they reject the Lord Jesus Christ — they themselves limit the universality of the atonement. It was put by Archbishop Ussher many years ago like this: "Christ died sufficiently for all, but efficiently only for the elect."[6]

How, then, does such a doctrine as this manage to affect the religious situation in the churches? How can such a doctrine, which to these opponents and critics seems so hard and narrow, such a limited doctrine, how can it encourage revival? — for that indeed was the effect it had when Spurgeon preached it. A study of the sermons preached during 1859 will provide us with the answer.

In the first place, although the preaching of Particular Redemption is doctrinal preaching, and although it is the preaching of a controversial doctrine, Spurgeon always felt that in preaching it he was offering to people the simplicity of the way of salvation. He said: "We too much omit the simple explanation of the essential act in salvation."[7] He continued: "I have feared that the anxious enquirer might visit many of our churches and chapels, month after month, and yet he would not get a clear idea of what he must do to be saved. He would come away with an indistinct notion that he was to believe, but what he was to believe he would not know. He would, perhaps obtain some glimmering of the fact that he must be saved through the merits of Christ, but how these merits can become available to him, he would still be left to guess."[8]

His aim, then, was to clarify the way of salvation so that his hearers might be in no doubt whatsoever what they must do to be saved. As he did when preaching upon the

[6] Parr, R., *Letters of Archbishop Ussher published by his Chaplain*, Nos. 22, 23.
[7] *New Park Street Pulpit*, 1859, p. 370.
[8] *Ibid.*

doctrine of Election, so when his theme was Particular Redemption he solved the difficulties of many.

He acknowledged many times that Particular Redemption was linked up with the sovereignty of God. Preaching the sermon entitled "Free Grace" in January, 1859, he said: "The reason why this day the Gospel is preached to you and not to the heathen far away, is not because, as a race, we are superior to the heathen; it is not because we deserve more at God's hands: His choice of Britain . . . is not caused by the excellency of the British nation, but entirely because of His own mercy and His own love. There is no reason in us why we should have the Gospel preached to us more than any other nation. Today, some of us have received the Gospel, and have been changed by it, and have become heirs of light and immortality, whereas others are left still to be the heirs of wrath. . . . But there is no reason *in us* why we should have been taken and others left."[9]

We might bring it up to date and say that the reason for having an open Bible and freedom of worship in Great Britain is not because we are morally better than the peoples of Russia or China, for instance. Indeed, it seems at the present time they have a higher ethical conception of sex, art and music than we have in this country; some of the degrading forms of these arts are not permitted in Russia. We are only a "peculiar people" in the sense of being favored by God of His sovereign will and purpose, not because of anything that we are in ourselves, or anything we have done. There is nothing in us as a nation, as a people, that merits us having this favor of God.

As Spurgeon put it in a later sermon called "The Shameful Sufferer," after reminding his congregation that it was their sins that crucified the Lord Jesus Christ as much as the sins of the Jews who called out "Crucify Him" and "Away with Him": "I know that we have pierced the Saviour; I know that we have crucified Him; and yet, strange

[9] *Ibid.*

to say, the blood which we fetched from those holy veins has washed us from our sins and has made us accepted in the beloved. . . . Now Jesus had to endure the stab in His inmost bowels, and to know that . . . His redeemed did it, that His own Church was His murderer — that His own people nailed Him to the tree."[10]

Since Spurgeon believed and preached a Gospel which won so many for the Lord Jesus Christ, and since he no more knew who were the particular ones to be redeemed in his congregation than he knew which were the elected ones, how was he able to preach that Christ died for the elect, for the particular ones, when he did not know who they were? He gave in his sermons what he called "a general call." He said, "The duty of the minister is to call souls to Christ, He is to make no distinction whatever."[11] But such a call "is not attended with Divine force and energy of the Holy Spirit in such a degree as to make it an unconquerable call, consequently men perish, even though they have the universal call of the Gospel ringing in their ears. The bell of God's house rings every day, sinners hear it, but they put their fingers in their ears, and they go their way, one to his farm, one to his merchandise, and though they are bidden and called to the wedding, yet they will not come, and by not coming they incur God's wrath, and He declareth of such — 'None of these men which were bidden shall taste of my supper.' The call of our text is of a different kind; it is not of a universal call; it is a special, particular, personal, discriminating, efficacious, unconquerable call. This call is sent to the predestined, and to them only; they by grace hear the call, obey it, and receive it. These are they who can now say, 'Draw us, and we will run after Thee.' "[12]

In a sermon entitled "Justice Satisfied" having twin texts, "For all have sinned, and come short of the glory of God"

[10] *Ibid.*, pp. 95, 96.
[11] *Ibid.*, p. 130.
[12] *Ibid.*

(Romans 3:27) and "If we confess our sins, He is faithful and righteous to forgive us our sins" (I John 1:9), Spurgeon declared that having punished Christ for human sin, God could not afterwards punish the sinner for it, for it would be unjust to demand two payments for one debt. "He cannot destroy the soul for whom Jesus died."[13] He continued in that sermon by having an imaginary conversation with a critic of his doctrine. "'Away goes universal redemption,' says one. Yes, away it goes, indeed. I am sure there is nothing about that in the Word of God. A redemption that does not redeem is not worth my preaching, or your hearing. Christ redeemed every soul that is saved; no more and no less. Every spirit that shall be seen in Heaven, Christ bought. If He had redeemed those in Hell, they never could have come there. He has bought His people with His blood, and they alone shall He bring with Him."[14]

He well knew that some of those who listened to his preaching week by week thought this view of redemption was a limited one, and so he concluded a sermon in October, 1859: "Remember, though you imagine, perhaps, from what I have been saying, that the Gospel is restricted, that the Gospel is freely preached to all. The decree is limited, but the good news is as wide as the world. The good news is as wide as the universe. I tell it to every creature under Heaven, because I am told to do so. The secret of God which is to deal with the application, that is restricted to God's chosen ones, but not the message, for that is to be proclaimed to all nations."[15]

That application of the Gospel to the particular ones for whom Christ died, Spurgeon declared, was the work of the Holy Spirit. Thus we see again how firm a Calvinist he was, for it was Calvin who emphasized the Spirit's work in salvation. In a sermon, "The Necessity of the Spirit's Work" (May, 1859), Spurgeon said:

[13] *Ibid.*, p. 245.
[14] *Ibid.*
[15] *Ibid.*, p. 424.

Take, again, the redemption of Christ. We know that Christ did stand in the room, place, and stead of all His people, and that all those who shall appear in heaven, will appear there as an act of justice as well as of grace, seeing that Christ was punished in their room and stead, and that it would have been unjust if God punished them, seeing that He had punished Christ for them. . . . But what avail is this to me, until the Spirit takes of the things of Christ and shows them to me? . . . There hang the blessings on the nail — on the nail Christ Jesus; but we are short of stature; we cannot reach them; the Spirit of God takes them down and gives them to us, and there they are; they are ours. . . . Without the Spirit we must die and perish just as much, though the Father elect and the Son redeem, as though the Father had never elected, and though the Son had never bought us with His blood. The Spirit is absolutely necessary. Without Him neither the works of the Father, nor of the Son, are of any avail to us.[16]

Such was his preaching during 1859. How unlike so much of our proclamation of the Gospel today! It was preaching that did not cheapen the Gospel. Neither did it result in superficiality among the converts. It honored God and enhanced His Word. It challenged men and women to solemn thinking and produced deep repentance in their hearts.

It is the fashion nowadays to make the way of salvation attractive. The Lord Jesus Christ never did that. He always told enquirers to count the cost. They were to sit down and make an honest assessment and see the real cost of becoming a Christian. He made Christianity something to be hardly won. A disciple was one who must never take his hand off the plough; he was a soldier for whom there was no discharge.

But today we try and make it easy. It is merely "follow the Lord Jesus Christ"; "decide for Him"; "exercise your will"; "do not bother about your past life, just look to the Lord Jesus Christ," and so we get converts with little or no spiritual depth and conspicuous lack of growth. They do not

[16] *Ibid.,* pp. 212, 213.

know what real repentance is. They have never been brought to tears because of their sins. Spurgeon made salvation attractive only in the sense of it being like a rare jewel that takes a lot of finding or fighting for until it is won. It was not a matter which could be taken or left. He often urged his people if they could not come to a decision there and then in the service to go home and in the quietness of their own room they were to think things out. He sometimes urged his hearers to go home alone if they possibly could, or if going home with a friend not to let them be overtalkative.

Twentieth century preaching is seriously lacking in anything thought-provoking like that. Many sermons are shallow and Christianity is made easy.

To those who thought his Calvinism was hard and unbending, Spurgeon had this personal word of testimony to say: "Well, if Christ never died for me, and never loved me, yet I must love Him for His goodness in dying for other people."[17] He felt that if even he were not one of the elect; if he were not one of the particular ones for whom Christ had died; he would still love Christ for dying for other people. But of course his contention was that no one can think like that without realizing that he is one of the particular ones Christ died to redeem.

D. Effectual Calling

We have already seen that when Spurgeon was preaching the Gospel, he declared that he was giving "a general call"; he relied on the Holy Spirit to make that call individual and effectual by application of the Gospel to the heart. Since no preacher knows those who are divinely elected or the particular ones whom Christ died to redeem, he has to be like Spurgeon and rely on the Holy Spirit's own ministry of applying the preached word to the individual heart. That, in essence, is the doctrine of effectual calling.

---

[17] Ibid., p. 488.

Calling, of course, is always associated in the Bible with the other Calvinistic doctrines. In Scripture the doctrine of effectual calling is closely linked with that of election, predestination, justification, salvation, glorification, in fact the whole process of salvation is indissolubly linked together. Thus we have such texts as these: "Many are called, but few are chosen" (Matthew 22:14); "Moreover whom he did predestinate, them he also called; and whom he called, them he also justified, and whom he justified, them he also glorified" (Romans 8:30); "(God) who hath called you unto his kingdom and glory" (I Thessalonians 2:12); "It pleased God, who . . . called me by his grace" (Galatians 1:15); "That hath called us to glory and virtue" (II Peter 1:8).

Of course, the Arminian also believes in giving a general call to the unconverted; but he believes that the call can be refused by the sinful listeners. The Calvinist, however, believes that since the call comes to the elect, it is irresistible, addressed to the heart, as it is, by the grace of the Sovereign God. Some call the general call "the external call," or "the common call," meaning that the sermon, the gospel message, as proclaimed by the preacher is extended to all mankind who come under the sound of it.

It is only too obvious in every gospel service or evangelistic campaign that when the Gospel is preached, and men and women are pleaded with regarding salvation and eternity, there does not seem to be a uniformity of influence. The New Testament teaches that only those respond who are recipients of God's "prevenient grace," as theologians call it, that is, anticipatory grace or grace that precedes repentance and conversion. We marvel at and praise God for those who come forward during an evangelistic campaign after an open appeal, but when we consider those untouched and unreached, both in that particular meeting, and Sunday by Sunday, there *is* no uniformity of influence, and it is only as we understand this doctrine of effectual calling that we can understand such a situation in our gospel services and campaigns.

A simple definition of effectual calling is this: "An exercise of Divine power upon the soul, immediate, spiritual, and supernatural, communicating a new spiritual life, and thus making a new mode of spiritual activity. (This) act of grace . . . can neither be co-operated with nor resisted."[1] It is not an effectual call because of the result, because someone has been saved. It is an effectual call because of its nature, because it is a divine call.

The chief objection to effectual calling by the opponents of Calvinism, and of course Spurgeon had many such opponents, is that the universal, common, external call which is given by the preacher must be insincere if those who reject it have not had the necessary or sufficient grace to enable them to respond to it. Dr. E. Y. Mullins answers this very satisfyingly: "Many a sincere invitation is given among men where it is known beforehand that it will not be accepted. Foreknowledge of a refusal does not affect the sincerity of the offer."[2]

Spurgeon, of course, was preaching on effectual calling in 1856, three years before the great revival year in the Music Hall,[3] but it was during 1859 that he taught the doctrine most regularly and effectively. He defined it as simply as this: "It finds the sinner dead, it gives him life, and he obeys the call of life and lives." He was preaching on "Predestination and Calling" from the text, "Moreover whom he did predestinate, them he also called: and whom he called, them he also justified: and whom he justified, them he also glorified" (Romans 8:30). He continued: "Every man that is saved, is always saved by an overcoming call which he cannot withstand; he may resist for a time, but he cannot resist so as to overcome it, he *must* give way, he *must* yield when God speaks. If He says, 'Let there be

---
[1] Hodge, A. A., *Outlines of Theology*, pp. 448, 449.
[2] *The Christian Religion in Its Doctrinal Expression*, p. 366.
[3] *New Park Street Pulpit*, 1856, No. 73 — *Effectual Calling*.

light,' the impenetrable darkness gives way to light; if He says, 'Let there be grace,' unutterable sin gives way, and the hardest-hearted sinner melts before the fire of effectual calling."[4]

As with the doctrine of election and particular redemption, Spurgeon saw that effectual calling was not dependent upon human merit. He said: "Now the calling of the Holy Spirit is without any regard to any merit in us. If this day the Holy Spirit shall call out of this congregation a hundred men, and bring them out of their estate of sin into a state of righteousness, you shall bring these hundred men, and let them march in review, and if you could read their hearts, you would be compelled to say, 'I see no reason why the Spirit of God should have operated upon these.' 'I see nothing whatever that could have merited such grace as this — nothing that could have caused the operations and motions of the Spirit to work in these men.' "[5]

No! it is not human merit. Effectual calling depends upon the sovereignty of God. Spurgeon was continually emphasizing that no one could be a Christian without God. In a sermon called "The Fainting Warrior," preached on January 23, 1859, he said: "I assure you . . . it is one of the hardest things in the world to be a child of God; in fact, it is impossible, unless the Lord makes us His children, and keeps us so."[6] In "Predestination and Calling," preached two months later, he used several Biblical illustrations of effectual calling. "The effectual call may be illustrated *in its sovereignty* by the case of Zacchaeus. Christ is entering into Jericho to preach. There is a publican living in it, who is a hard, griping, grasping, miserly extortioner. Jesus Christ is coming in to call someone, for it is written that He must abide in some man's house. Would you believe that the man whom Christ intends to call is the worst man in Jericho — the extortioner? . . . Now why call Zacchaeus?

[4] *Ibid.*, 1859, p. 131.
[5] *Ibid.*, p. 68.
[6] *Ibid.*, p. 85.

There were many better men in the city than he. Why call him? Simply because the call of God comes to unworthy sinners. There is nothing in man that can deserve this call; nothing in the best of men that can invite it: but God quickeneth whom He will, and when He sends that call, though it come to the vilest of the vile, down they come speedily and swiftly; they come down from the tree of their sin, and fall prostrate in penitence at the feet of Jesus Christ."[7]

In that same sermon he used several other Scriptural examples of divine, sovereign, effectual calling. The case of Lazarus was cited to emphasize that salvation is all of God and His grace, that it is not dependent upon human merit, effort or assistance. There is nothing we can do to be raised from spiritual death. We cannot even assist God in this work, for it is His alone. Spurgeon said: "The sister of that corrupt body stands at the side of the tomb, and she says, 'Lord, by this time he stinketh; for he hath been dead four days.' This is the voice of reason and of nature. Martha is correct; but by Martha's side there stands a man who, despite all His lowliness, is Very God of Very God. . . . 'Loose him and let him go,' saith the Redeemer; and then he walks in all the liberty of life. The effectual call of grace is precisely similar; the sinner is dead in sin; he is not only in sin but dead in sin, without any power whatever to give to himself the life of grace. . . . Sovereign Mercy comes, and there lies this unconscious, lifeless mass of sin. Sovereign Grace cries, either by the minister, or else directly without any agency, by the Spirit of God, 'Come forth!' and that man lives. Does he contribute anything to his new life? Not he; his life is given solely by God. He was dead, absolutely dead, rotten in his sin; the life is given when the call comes, and, in obedience to the call, the sinner comes forth from the grave."[8]

Illustrating the effect of this divine call to life, Spur-

[7] *Ibid.*, p. 132.
[8] *Ibid.*, p. 130.

geon gave an Old Testament illustration, Abraham leaving home and journeying "not knowing whither he went." The preacher declared: "When God called Abraham, he called him alone and blessed him out of Ur of the Chaldees, and said to him, 'Go forth, Abraham,' and he went forth, not knowing whither he went. Now, when effectual calling comes into a house and singles out a man, that man will be compelled to go forth without the camp, bearing Christ's reproach. He must come out from his very dearest friends, from all his old acquaintances, from those friends with whom he used to drink, swear, and take pleasure; he must go straight away from them all, to follow the Lamb whithersoever he goeth.... Man! if thou art called, if thou art called truly, there will be a going out, and a going out alone.... But if it be an effectual call, and if salvation shall be the result thereof, what matters it that thou dost go to heaven alone?"[9]

Samuel was cited to emphasize that at first a man may be unaware that he is being called with effectual calling. Spurgeon said in the same sermon:

> When effectual calling comes to a man, at first he may not know that it is effectual calling. You remember the case of Samuel; the Lord called Samuel, and he arose and went to Eli, and he said, "Here am I, for thou calledst me." Eli said, "I called not, lie down again." And he went and lay down. The second time the Lord called him and said "Samuel, Samuel," and he arose again, and went to Eli, and said, "Here am I, for thou didst call me," and then it was that Eli, not Samuel, first perceived that the Lord had called the child. And when Samuel knew it was the Lord, he said, "Speak; for thy servant heareth." When the work of grace begins in the heart a man is not always clear that it is God's work; he is impressed under the minister, and perhaps he is rather more occupied with the impression than with the agent of the impression; he said, "I know not how it is, but I have been called; Eli, the minister, has called me." And perhaps he goes to Eli and asks what he wants with him. "Surely," said he, "the minister knew me, and spoke something personally

[9] *Ibid.*, p. 132.

to me, because he knew my case." And he goes to Eli, and it is not till afterwards, perhaps, that he finds that Eli had nothing to do with the impression, but that the Lord had called him. . . . I may say to those who are the beginners in the divine life, so long as your call is real, rest assured that it is Divine. . . . If the call be effectual, and you are brought out and brought in — brought out of sin and brought to Christ, brought out of death into life, and out of slavery into liberty, then, though thou canst not see God's hand in it, yet it is there.[10]

Since one may be unaware in the early stages that it is divine calling, how may a sinner be absolutely sure? What is the answer to self-deception, delusion, or even hallucination? For Spurgeon there had to be serious self-examination in the light of certain Scriptures. He said, "If in your Bibles you turn to II Timothy 1:9, you read these words — 'Who hath saved us, and called us with an holy calling.' Now here is the first touchstone by which we may try our calling — many are called but few are chosen, because there are many kinds of call, but the true call, and that only, answers to the description of the text. It is 'an holy calling, not according to our works, but according to His own purpose and grace, and was given us in Christ Jesus before the world began.' This calling forbids all trust in our own doings and conducts us to Christ alone for salvation, but it afterwards purges us from dead works to serve the living and true God. If you are living in sin, you are not called; if you can still continue as you were before your pretended conversion, then it is no conversion at all."[11]

Referring to Philippians 3:13 and 14, Spurgeon asked his hearers: "Is then your calling a high calling, has it lifted up your heart, and set it upon Heavenly things? Has it lifted up your hopes, to hope no longer for things that are on earth, but for things that are above? Has it lifted up your tastes, so that they are no longer grovelling, but you choose the things that are of God? Has it lifted up your desires, so

[10] *Ibid.*, pp. 132, 133.
[11] *Ibid.*, p. 133.

that you are panting not for earthly things, but for things that are not seen and are eternal? Has it lifted up the constant tenor of your life, so that you spend your life with God in prayer, and praise, and thanksgiving, and can no longer be satisfied with the low and mean pursuits which you followed in the days of your ignorance? Recollect, if you are truly called, it is a high calling, a calling from on high, and a calling that lifts up your heart, and raises it to the high things of God, eternity, heaven and holiness."[12]

In Hebrews 3:1 Spurgeon saw proof of effectual calling. "Heavenly calling means a call *from* heaven. Have you been called, not of man, but of God? Can you now detect in your calling, the hand of God, and the voice of God? If man alone call thee, thou art uncalled. Is thy calling of God? And is it a call *to* heaven as well as *from* heaven?"[13]

After quoting and commenting upon several more Scriptural passages, Spurgeon declared: "Let me say now, before I turn from this point, that it is possible for a man to know whether God has called him or not, and he may know it too, beyond a doubt. He may know it as surely as if he had read it with his own eyes; nay, he may know it more surely than that, for if I read a thing with my eyes, even my eyes may deceive me, the testimony of sense may be false, but *the testimony of the Spirit must be true*. We have the witness of the Spirit within, bearing witness with our spirits that we are born of God. . . . What would some of you give if you could arrive at this assurance? Mark, if you anxiously desire to know, you may know. If your heart pants to read its title clear it shall do so ere long. . . . Ask for assurance; and when thou gettest assurance, ask for full assurance; and when thou hast obtained full assurance, ask for enjoyment; and when thou hast enjoyment, ask for glory itself; and He shall surely give it thee in its appointed season."[14]

[12] *Ibid.*
[13] *Ibid.*
[14] *Ibid.*, pp. 134, 135.

Once definite assurance of the believer's calling had been given, then according to Spurgeon his calling was further proof of his Divine Election. Spurgeon preached on "The Necessity of the Spirit's Work" (May, 1859): "Election is a dead letter both in my consciousness and in any effect which it can produce upon me, until the Spirit of God calls me out of darkness into marvellous light. And then through my calling, I see my election, and knowing myself to be called of God, I know myself to have been chosen of God from before the foundation of the world. . . . Until the Spirit opens the eyes to read, until the Spirit imparts the mystic secret no heart can know its election."[15]

In "Predestination and Calling" he declared: "O my hearer, by thy name I know thee not, and by thy name God's Word doth not declare thee, but by thy character thou mayest read thy name; and if thou hast been a partaker of the calling which is mentioned in the text, then mayest thou conclude beyond a doubt that thou art among the predestined — 'For whom he did predestinate them he also called.' And if thou be called, it follows as a natural inference thou art predestined."[16]

The emphasis upon the Holy Spirit's work we have already seen is characteristic of Calvin and his followers. Spurgeon repeatedly affirmed that effectual calling was the work of the Holy Spirit. He would end a sermon with such words as: "O Spirit of the Living God, draw them now!" yet, acknowledging God's use of the human agent, would always add: "Let these feeble weak words be the means of drawing souls to Christ."[17] On another occasion he ended: "O Spirit, bring sinners to Thyself . . . O may the Spirit make my appeal effectual!"[18]

From personal testimony he was able to pay tribute to the work of the Holy Spirit in calling sinners to repentance,

[15] *Ibid.*, p. 212.
[16] *Ibid.*, p. 129.
[17] *Ibid.*, p. 72.
[18] *Ibid.*, p. 448.

faith and salvation. He ended a sermon entitled "The Sweet Uses of Adversity" with these words: "I will tell you how I came to believe. Once upon a time I was trying to make myself believe, and a voice whispered, 'Vain man, vain man, if thou wouldest believe come and see!' Then the Holy Spirit led me by the hand to a solitary place. And while I stood there, suddenly there appeared before me One upon His Cross. I looked up, I had then no faith. I saw His eyes suffused with tears, and the blood still flowing; I saw His enemies about Him hunting Him to the grave; I marked His miseries unutterable; I heard the groaning which cannot be described; and as I looked up, He opened His eyes and said to me, 'The Son of man is come into the world to seek and to save that which was lost.' I clapped my hands, and said, 'Jesus, I do believe, I must believe what Thou hast said. I could not believe before, but the sight of Thee has breathed faith into my soul. I dare not doubt — it were treason, it were high treason to doubt Thy power to save.' Dissolved by agonies, I fell on the ground, and embraced His feet, and when I fell my sin fell also."[19]

For Spurgeon, the Holy Spirit called in various ways, each call as effectual as another, for each was suited to the individual need, but a call through the cross of Calvary seemed to be the most common. In a sermon entitled "Who Can Tell?" (September, 1859) he drew a parallel between the people of Nineveh receiving God's warning through the prophet Jonah and the people of all ages who receive spiritual warnings from God's ministers and preachers. He proclaimed: "The voice from the Cross is speaking, and each trickling drop of blood crieth, 'Amen.' "[20]

The call also came through the Word. It has already been seen that Spurgeon placed great importance on the Bible as a means of assurance to believers of their call, but

[19] *Ibid.*, p. 472.
[20] *Ibid.*, p. 406.

they also called unbelievers effectually. "Oh! hear the word of the Gospel, ere ye separate, for the Spirit speaketh effectually to you now in this short sentence — 'Repent and be converted every one of you, that your sins may be blotted out,' . . . and hear this solemn sentence — 'He that believeth in the Lord Jesus, and is baptized shall be saved; but he that believeth not shall be damned.' "[21]

The problem as to why the call seems unanswered in so many cases was solved by Spurgeon in the following manner: "How many of you have been called under the sound of the ministry and yet you have not come? Why is it? . . . Why do you not come? . . . Surely if you will not come at the Saviour's bidding, you will not come at mine. If your own stern necessities do not make you attend to His gracious call, surely nothing I can say can ever move you. . . . O, Saviour! call ye them effectually. Call now; let the Spirit speak. O Spirit of the living God, bid the poor prisoner come, and let him leap to loose his chains. I know that which kept me a long time from the Saviour was the idea that He had never called me; and yet when I came to Him, I discovered that long ere that He had invited me, but I had closed my ear; I thought surely He had invited every one else to Him, but I must be left out, the poorest and the vilest of them all. O sinner, if such be thy consciousness, then you are one to whom the invitation is specially addressed."[22]

Just as the doctrine of election did not lead to sinful living in Spurgeon's eyes, so the doctrine of effectual calling did not lead to laziness. He had no time for the man who said, "If God intends to save me, I need do nothing."[23] He answered such an attitude by saying: "He knows he is a fool when he says it; or if he does not know it, I will soon

[21] *Ibid.*, p. 422.
[22] *Ibid.*, pp. 334, 335.
[23] *Ibid.*, p. 57.

make him see it. Suppose he says again, 'If the Lord intends to feed me he will feed me, and I will go without my dinner? If the Lord intends to give me a harvest, He will give me a harvest, and I shall not sow any wheat, and I shall not plough.' Suppose another were to say, 'If the Lord intends to keep me warm today, he will do it; so I will not put on my coat.' Suppose a man should say again, 'If the Lord intends me to go to bed tonight, I shall go to bed; and, therefore, I shall not walk towards home, but sit here as long as I like.' You smile at once, because the folly is self-convincing. But is it not just the same in religion? Because 'the Lord will perfect that which concerneth me' am I to say I shall not pray? Why, no, my dear friends, the fact is, that a knowledge that a thing is certain prompts a wise man to action."[24]

Such was Spurgeon's confidence in God, His sovereignty and wisdom, His power and prevenient grace, that as he preached he prayed and expected God to call effectually before the sermon was ended.

"I trust that even while I am preaching this morning, Christ may speak with me, and some word that may fall from my lips, unpremeditated and almost without design, shall be sent of God as a message of life unto some dead and corrupt heart here, and some man who has lived in sin hitherto, shall now live to righteousness, live to Christ."[25] That was the kind of prayer which he prayed while he was actually preaching. That is the kind of prayer which we need from those who listen to whom the effectual call has already come. That is the kind of prayer that church members need to pray while their minister is preaching. We need to pray every time the Gospel is preached that God in His sovereignty and wisdom will send forth the call which is effectual not first because of the result but because it is His own divine call.

[24] *Ibid.*, p. 57.
[25] *Ibid.*, p. 131.

E. FINAL PERSEVERANCE

The simplest definition of this doctrine would be the cliché that is given to so many converts after our gospel services or evangelistic campaigns: "Once saved, always saved." That is the doctrine which Spurgeon preached under the title of The Final Perseverance of the Saints. The word "perseverance" has rather changed its meaning over the years, just as we have seen that terms like Total Depravity, and Particular and Peculiar have also varied in meaning.

Whereas today we look upon the word "persevere" as meaning "being steadfast" or "constant," that is, a continuing process, the word originally had more the force of fact or condition. Theologically it has always meant — continuance in a state of grace leading to a final state of glory. And so when we speak of perseverance it is really God's perseverance of the saints and not the saints' own perseverance. Perhaps it is better to use the word preservation — God's preservation of the saints.

A better phrase than "once saved, always saved" is "eternal security," and that is the word which theologians tend to use more today — the eternal security of the believer. At any rate Spurgeon's belief was that after salvation there is a perseverance, a preservation, a continuance in that divine grace which saved us, now working out our salvation through sanctification until glorification takes place. Salvation then is an everlasting salvation; those saved cannot possibly be lost, declares this doctrine. Text upon text can be quoted to uphold this view and also lengthy Bible passages such as Romans 8.

Without going into detailed explanation of contrary texts to this doctrine, we may say that in general the texts which seem to deny the doctrine are those which really deal with spurious conversions, a pretended, a superficial, nominal one. They are really dealing with those who merely have an outward profession, perhaps of church-going, of outward Christian morality, or the giving of their gifts to good causes rather than an inner Holy Spirit experience. As T. C. Hammond puts it: "There is a greater number of allusions and far more positive statements on the side of eternal security. It should be also noted that the Scriptures on the other side are mostly negative and in the nature of warnings not to presume."[1] He adds: Hebrews 6:4-6 and 10:26, 27, for instance, may be taken "as hypothetical cases, stated for the purposes of argument."[2]

The doctrine of the final perseverance of the saints then is that Christ not only saves, but He keeps; and He not only keeps, but one day He will present us faultless before the Throne of God's glory in heaven (Jude 24).

In the face of such glorious teaching, containing such comfort for the struggling believer, such encouragement for weak and feeble saints, it seems difficult to believe that so many have scorned Calvinism and criticized it for being hard and restrictive. Bitter controversy has, however, raged over this fifth point of Calvinism. It divided George Whitefield from John Wesley; it divides the "Salvationist" and many Methodists from other Christians today. These people speak of "falling from grace," or "selling one's birthright." The Arminian believes that a Christian can "commit spiritual suicide," or that one who has been "born again" can be "unborn"!

It is seen at once how such a doctrine is at variance with the logic and emphasis of Calvinism. According to the Calvinist, the saved man is an elect one, chosen of God through His sovereign grace; and as such an object of divine grace and mercy he cannot be lost eternally. As long as we begin with divine sovereignty, then final perseverance follows; but begin with human freedom and free-will and it is possible to contemplate this awful process of falling from grace.

The relevant Scripture texts teaching the doctrine of

[1] *In Understanding Be Men*, p. 195.
[2] *Ibid.*

final perseverance are — Romans 8:29-39; John 6:37; John 10:28, 29; I Peter 1:5, 8, 9; Philippians 1:6; II Timothy 1:12.

T. C. Hammond quotes from H. C. G. Moule: "It is remarkable that in the definitely chosen biographies of Scripture no person appears who, at one time certainly a Saint of God, at a later time was certainly a lost man."[3]

Attempts have been made, of course, to combine the two views, but this is rather like trying to mix oil and water.

The chief objection to the doctrine is the one offered against the doctrine of election, that it must lead to careless living. The Bible does not allow this, however. The emphasis is always upon constant watchfulness, diligence, and prayer. Although a man is assured that his salvation is eternal, he is still one who has to "fight the good fight of faith."

Spurgeon preached a number of sermons upon this particular doctrine. In the complete index to his sermons published in the volumes of *The Metropolitan Tabernacle Pulpit* there are ten sermons listed under the title "Final Perseverance (Preservation) of the Saints." In many others he taught the doctrine incidentally. Before the revival year of 1859 he preached upon it, devoting the whole of one sermon to the doctrine (*The New Park Street Pulpit*, No. 73).

During 1859, when revival reached Great Britain, the year that Spurgeon saw such spiritual prosperity on his ministry in the Surrey Gardens Music Hall, he stressed emphatically the difference between the Arminian and the Calvinist on this subject: "The Calvinist holds, that none can perish for whom Jesus died — that His blood was never shed in vain, and that of all those of whom He hath redeemed, none shall ever perish. The Arminian teaches that though a man should be regenerated and become a child of God today, he may tomorrow be cast out of the covenant, and be as much a child of the devil

[3] *Ibid.*, p. 196.

as if no spiritual change had been wrought in him. 'Not so,' says the Calvinist, 'salvation is of God alone, and where once He begins He never leaves off, until He has finished the good work.' "[4] It is rather like the man who was reputed to have been saved at a Salvation Army open air meeting and then went to his usual public house and became drunk. He went to the citadel on Sunday and was saved again, but on the Monday he was once more in his cups — and so it went on, alternative periods of sobriety and drunkenness, until his wife prayed: "Lord, when you take him, take him when he's sober!" That is the difficulty in which the Arminian doctrine places people. Here is this man alternatively saved and lost, if he dies while he is lost, he is lost forever.

For Spurgeon that was utterly impossible, because God was "the author and finisher of our faith" (Hebrews 12:2). He said: "Not only are you not condemned, but you never shall be."[5]

He illustrated final perseverance from the factory: "You sometimes see in a factory the wheels running some this way, and some the other, and some cross-ways, and they seem to be playing all sorts of antics, but somehow or other the deviser brings them all to work for some settled object. And I know that come prosperity or come adversity, come sickness or come health, come foe, come friend, come popularity, or come contempt, His purpose shall be worked out, and that purpose shall be pure, unmingled good to every blood-bought heir of mercy on whom His heart is set."[6]

Running on all through Spurgeon's teaching and preaching of this doctrine is the Calvinistic emphasis of the sovereignty of God. He said: "God's people, after they are called by grace, are preserved in Christ Jesus; they are 'kept by the power of God through faith unto salvation'; they are not suffered to sin away their eternal inheritance, but as

[4] *New Park Street Pulpit*, 1859, p. 111.
[5] *Ibid.*, p. 80.
[6] *Ibid.*, p. 296.

temptations arise they have strength given them with which to encounter them, and as sin blackens them they are washed afresh and again cleansed. But mark, the reason why God keeps His people is the same as that which made them His people — His own free sovereign grace."[7] Or, as he had stressed in earlier sermons that year, preaching on "Faith in Perfection" from the text, "The Lord will perfect that which concerneth me" (Psalm 138:8): *"The Lord* will perfect that which concerneth me. And O Christian, if thou hast any confidence which is not grounded on the Lord and rooted in the Rock of Ages, thy confidence is worse than a dream, it shall deceive thee, pierce thee, wound thee, and cast thee down to thine own future sorrow and grief."[8]

Scriptural proof was always ready to hand for Spurgeon. In "Predestination and Calling" (preached on March 6, 1859) he declared: "If a man be called he will certainly be saved at last. To prove that, however, I will refer you to the express words of Scripture: Romans 11:29 — 'For the gifts and calling of God are without repentance.' He never repents of what He gives, nor of what He calls."[9]

As with Election, Particular Redemption and Effectual Calling, when considering the believer's eternal security Spurgeon would not allow human merit to enter into it. We are not preserved or kept because of anything in us, or because of anything we are or do. "The only reason," he said in a sermon entitled "Free Grace" (January, 1859), "why God shall bring us to Heaven shall be His own love, and not because we deserve it."[10] In "Faith in Perfection" he said: "The believer is sure he shall be saved. Why? Because of his merits? No! Because of the strength of his own faith? No! Because he has something which will recommend him to God? No; he believes he shall be perfected because of God's mercy."[11] Later the same year, he said:

[7] *Ibid.*, p. 68.
[8] *Ibid.*, p. 51.
[9] *Ibid.*, p. 135.
[10] *Ibid.*, p. 68.
[11] *Ibid.*, p. 55.

"If your perseverance depends upon yourself, you are a lost man. You may write that down for a certainty. If you have one jot or one tittle to do with your own perseverance in Divine Grace, you will never see God's face at last; your grace will die out; your life will be extinguished, and you must perish, if your salvation depends upon yourself."[12]

Not only was there nothing meritorious in the believer to persuade God to be favorable, but the Christian was quite incapable of making himself eternally secure through his own efforts, in the same way that he had no ability to repent, or have faith, or be converted. Preaching a sermon entitled, upon publication, "Faith Illustrated," Spurgeon declared in August of the revival year: "Paul! art thou sure that thou canst keep thyself? 'No,' says he, 'I have nothing to do with that': and yet thou art sure of thy salvation! 'Yes,' saith he, 'I am.' How is it then? 'Why, I am persuaded that *He* is able to keep me. Christ, to whom I commit myself, I know hath power enough to hold me to the end.' Martin Luther was bold enough to exclaim, 'Let him that died for my soul see to the salvation of it.' "[13] Then followed a tremendous passage in that same sermon, in which Spurgeon catechized the Apostle Paul about his eternal security. Neither hunger, thirst, being forsaken by others, burning at the stake, offered tempting riches or position, nothing would make Jesus give up Paul. The apostle might be tempted to renounce Christ, but Christ would keep him.

We should expect some reference to be made by Spurgeon to the Holy Spirit's work in the saints' final perseverance. In a sermon on "Grieving the Holy Spirit" (October, 1859) Spurgeon took as his text Ephesians 4:30 — "And grieve not the Holy Spirit of God, whereby ye are sealed unto the day of redemption." He explained the term "sealed" by saying that it stood for attestation, appropriation and preservation. "It is possible for a man to know infallibly

[12] *Ibid.*, p. 175.
[13] *Ibid.*, p. 375.

that he is secure of heaven. He may not only hope so, but he may know it beyond a doubt, and he may know it thus — by being able with the eye of faith to use the seal, the broad stamp of the Holy Spirit set upon his own character and experience. It is a seal of attestation."[14] Speaking of sealing meaning preservation, he declared: "Men seal up that which they wish to have preserved, and when a document is sealed it becomes valid henceforth. Now it is by the Spirit of God that the Christian is sealed, that he is kept, he is preserved, sealed unto the day of redemption — sealed until Christ comes fully to redeem the world by purging it from sin, and making it a kingdom unto Himself in righteousness. We shall hold on our way; we shall be saved. The chosen people cannot be lost, they must be brought home at last. By the sealing of the Spirit. Apart from that they perish; they are undone. When the last general fire shall blaze out, everything that has not the seal of the Spirit on it, shall be burned up. But the men on whose forehead is the seal shall be preserved."[15]

Doubt as to this doctrine of final preservation Spurgeon knew would cripple the believer's life and testimony, and so in the sermon, "Mr. Fearing Comforted," preached in April, 1859, on the text, "O thou of little faith, wherefore didst thou doubt?" (Matthew 14:31), he said that he knew "many ... of God's people who are much vexed and troubled with doubts about their present acceptance."[16] He put it down to self-examination that concluded: "Look, what an evil heart of unbelief I have; I cannot live one day without sin; my heart is so treacherous, it is like a bombshell; let but a spark of temptation fall upon it and it will blow up to my eternal destruction. With such a tinder box as I have, how can I hope to escape, while I walk in the midst of a shower of sparks?"[17]

[14] *Ibid.*, p. 429.
[15] *Ibid.*
[16] *Ibid.*, p. 173.
[17] *Ibid.*, p. 175.

Or other Christians falsely concluded, he said: "I feel my nature to be so utterly vile and depraved that I cannot hope to persevere. If I hold on a week or a month it will be a great work; but to hold on all my life until I die — oh! this is impossible."[18]

Yes, it is habitually and wilfully falling into sin that makes us doubt the truth of this doctrine. Spurgeon was well aware of this. His answer was: "(God's mercy) endureth all the weight of sin; it endureth for ever. But what if we should live in sin so long that at last God denied mercy to us even though we believe in Him? That cannot be; we cannot sin longer than for ever — His mercy cannot be tried longer, and even if it could be tried for ever it would endure for ever. All the weight of my trouble, all the weight of my backsliding, all the weight of my evil heart of unbelief — all the everlasting arches of Divine mercy can and will sustain. Those arches never shall rock; the stone never shall be crumbled; it shall never be swept away by even the floods of eternity itself. Because His mercy endureth for ever, God will most assuredly perfect the work of His hands."[19]

For himself, believing that a few ounces of personal testimony were worth more than many pounds of theory, he said: "I am certain of the doctrine of Final Perseverance, because I have persevered as long as I have. If God meant to take my name out of the covenant, he has had good reasons enough long ere this."[20] He believed in *final* perseverance because he was enjoying *present* perseverance. As he said in April, 1859: "Remember, you have already been kept these months, and these years: what has done that? Why, Divine grace; and the Divine grace that has held you on for one year can hold you on for a century, nay, for an eternity, if it were necessary."[21]

[18] *Ibid.*
[19] *Ibid.*, p. 56.
[20] *Ibid.*, p. 230.
[21] *Ibid.*, p. 175.

In a descriptive and dramatic passage in "The Believer's Challenge," preached in June, 1859, he spoke of the end of the world. Amidst terrible happenings and terrifying experiences, he said the believer would stand safe and secure: "I see the heavens on fire, rolling up like a scroll — I see sun, moon, stars pale now their feeble light — the earth is tottering, the pillars of heaven are rocking; the grand assize is commenced — the herald angels descend, not to sing this time, but with thundering trumpets to proclaim, 'He comes, He comes to judge the earth in righteousness and the people in equity.' What says the believer now? He says, 'I fear not that assize, for who can condemn?' The great white throne is set, the books are opened, men are trembling, fiends are yelling, sinners are shrieking — 'Rocks hide, mountains on us fall.' These make up an awful chorus of dismay. There stands the believer, and looking round on the assembled universe of men and angels, he cries, 'Who shall lay anything to my charge?' and silence reigns through earth and heaven. . . . Christ will not belie Himself. He cannot reverse His grace; it cannot be that the throne of condemnation shall be exalted on the ruins of the Cross."[22]

What a doctrine to declare in the face of threatened nuclear warfare! How necessary it is to proclaim it, when on every side men's hearts are failing them for fear — Eternal Security! — not the security offered by a welfare state, but when the very heavens seem to be falling through the rocking of the world's foundations because of man's own madness and inhumanity to man; to be able to tell them how they can be eternally secure — what a Gospel!

For Spurgeon there was no other doctrine worth preaching. Of the Arminian view he said in "Dilemma and Deliverance" (one of the last sermons to be delivered in the Music Hall, in December, 1859): "If we can but once believe the doctrine that the child of God may fall from grace and perish everlastingly, we might indeed shut up our Bible

---

[22] *Ibid.*, p. 256.

in despair. To what purpose would my preaching be — the preaching of a rickety gospel like that? To what purpose your faith — a faith in a God that cannot and would not carry on to the end? To what use the blood of Christ, if it were shed in vain, and did not bring the blood-bought securely home? To what purpose the Spirit, that if He were not omnipotent enough to overcome our wandering, to arrest our sins and make us perfect, and present us faultless before the throne of God at last? That doctrine of the final perseverance of the saints is, I believe, as thoroughly bound up with the standing or falling of the Gospel, as is the article of justification by faith. . . . An unchanging God, an everlasting covenant, a sure mercy, these are the things that my soul delights in."[23] Yet there are some who dearly hold on to this doctrine of eternal security and shun the other four points of Calvinism. Many do not believe in election or predestination or calling, yet like the comfort of eternal security. They have obviously overlooked the logic of Calvin's system, or they have failed to see the sovereignty of God running through every one of the five points.

This was a doctrine which Spurgeon accepted as a young believer. "A few months after I first sought and found salvation, I enjoyed the sweet privilege of full assurance. . . . I expressed myself very confidently concerning the great truth that God would ne'er forsake His people, nor leave His work undone."[24] In fact, he said he was as confident as the Psalmist who "had no more doubt about his own ultimate perfection, than he had about his existence."[25] No wonder then that he could utter such an appeal for belief in eternal security at the end of a sermon as this: "Oh! believe that thou art secure; that voice which called thee, shall call thee yet again from earth to heaven, from death's dark gloom to immortality's unutterable splendours; rest assured, the heart that called thee, beats with infinite love

[23] *Ibid.*, 1860, p. 12.
[24] *Ibid.*, 1859, p. 53.
[25] *Ibid.*

towards thee, a love undying that many waters cannot quench, and that floods cannot drown. Sit thee down, rest in peace; lift up thine eye of hope, and sing thy song with fond anticipation. Thou shalt soon be with the glorified, where thy portion is; thou art only waiting here to be made meet for the inheritance, and that done, the wings of angels shall waft thee far away, to the mount of peace, and joy, and blessedness, where —

> 'Far from a world of grief and sin,
> With God eternally shut in.' "[26]

[26] *Ibid.*, p. 136.

ADDENDUM TO CHAPTER TWO

Besides preaching about revival during 1859, and also proclaiming the doctrines that fell upon the congregation with revival blessing, in several sermons Spurgeon described the American revival and the awakening then in progress in Ireland. His accounts confirm what later historians, such as Dr. J. Edwin Orr, have discovered from other sources.

In July, 1859, he preached in the Music Hall a sermon titled "The Story of God's Mighty Acts" (text, Psalm 44:1). After reviewing revivals under the apostle Peter, Martin Luther, Whitefield and Wesley, which he called "the works of God in the olden time,"[1] he went on to illustrate how all the mighty works of God have been attended with great prayer."[2] He said, "Have ye ever heard of the commencement of the great American revival? A man unknown and obscure, laid it up in his heart to pray that God would bless his country. After praying and wrestling and making the soul-stirring enquiry, 'Lord, what wilt thou have *me* to do? Lord what wilt thou have me *to do?*' he hired a room, and put up an announcement that there would be a prayer-meeting held there at such-and-such an hour of the day. He went at the proper hour, and there was not a single person there; he began to pray, and prayed for half-an-hour alone. One came in at the end of the half-hour, and then two more, and I think he closed with six. The next week came round, and there might have been fifty dropped in at different times; at last the prayer meeting grew to a hundred, then others began to start prayer meetings; at last there was scarcely a street in New York that was without a prayer meeting. Merchants found time to run in, in the

[1] *New Park Street Pulpit,* 1859, p. 307.
[2] *Ibid.,* p. 309.

middle of the day to pray. The prayer meetings became daily ones, lasting for about an hour; petitions and requests were sent up, these were simply asked and offered before God, and the answers came; and many were the happy hearts that stood up and testified that the prayer offered last week had been already fulfilled. Then it was when they were all in earnest prayer, suddenly the Spirit of God fell upon the people, and it was rumoured that in a certain village a preacher had been preaching in thorough earnest, and there had been hundreds converted in a week. The matter spread into and through the Northern States — these revivals of religion became universal, and it has been sometimes said, that a quarter of a million of people were converted to God through the short space of two or three months."[3] Such then was his description of what we now call the Fulton Street Prayer Meeting and its effect upon American Christians and churches.

Turning to the revival that reached Irish shores from across the Atlantic, Spurgeon said: "Now the same effect was produced in Ballymena and Belfast by the same means. The brother thought that it lay at his heart to pray, and he did pray, then he held a regular prayer meeting, day after day they met together to entreat the blessing, and the fire descended and the work was done. Sinners were converted, not by ones or twos, but by hundreds and thousands, and the Lord's name was greatly magnified by the progress of the Gospel. Beloved, I am only telling you *facts*. Make each of you your own estimate of them if you please."[4]

It was not until November of that year that Spurgeon again spoke at length upon a specific revival of his own day. Once more he was emphasizing prayer. The sermon was entitled "Let Us Pray," and after urging his hearers to pray more for God's blessing upon all Christian work, he said:

[3] *Ibid.*
[4] *Ibid.*

APPENDUM TO CHAPTER II

I will tell you here an incident of the revival. It is one I know to be correct; it is told by a good brother who would not add a word thereunto, I am sure. It happened, not long ago, that in a school which is sustained by the Corporation of the City of London, in the north of Ireland, one of the bigger boys had been converted to God; and one day, in the midst of school, a younger youth was greatly oppressed by a sense of sin, and so overwhelmed did he become that the master plainly perceived that he could not work, and therefore he said to him, "You had better go home, and plead with God in prayer, in private." He said, however, to the bigger boy, who was all rejoicing in hope, "Go with him; take him home and pray with him." They started together: on the road they saw an empty house; the two boys went in and there began to pray; the plaintive cry of the young one, after a little time changed into a note of joy, when, suddenly springing up, he said, "I have found rest in Jesus; I have never felt as I do now; my sins, which are many, are all forgiven."

The proposal was to go home; but the lad forbade this. No, he must go and tell the master of the school that he had found Christ. So hurrying back, he rushed in and said: "Oh! I have found the Lord Jesus Christ." All the boys in the school, who had seen him sitting sad and dull upon the form, remarked the joy that flashed from his eye, when he cried, "I have Christ." The effect was electric. The boys suddenly and mysteriously disappeared; the master knew not where they were gone; but looking over into the playground, he saw by the wall were a number of boys, one by one, in prayer asking for mercy. He said to the older youth, "Cannot you go and tell these boys the way of salvation — tell them what they must do to be saved?" He did so, and the silent prayer was suddenly changed into a loud, piercing shriek; the boys in the school understood it, and, impelled by the Great Spirit, they all fell on their knees, and began to cry aloud for mercy through the blood of Christ.

But this was not all. There was a girls' schoolroom in the same building overhead. The ear had been well tutored to understand what that cry meant, and soon interpreted it, and the girls, too, affected by the same Spirit, fell down and began to cry aloud for the forgiveness of their sins. Here was an interruption of the school! Was ever such a thing known before in a school-room? Classes are all put aside, books forgotten; everything cast to the winds, while poor sinners are kneeling at the foot of the cross seeking for pardon. The cry was heard throughout the various offices attached to this large school, and it was heard also across the street, and passers-by were attracted — men of God, ministers and clergymen of the neighbourhood were brought in — the whole day was spent in prayer, and they continued until almost midnight; but they separated with songs of joy, for that vast mass of girls and boys, men and women, who had crowded the two schoolrooms, had all found the Saviour.[5]

As evidence of the reality of that school revival Spurgeon went on in the same sermon to tell how a friend (Dr. Arthur) "met with a youth while travelling in Ireland, and he said to him, 'Do you love the Saviour?' And he said 'I trust I do.' 'How did you come to love Him?' 'Oh,' he said, 'I was converted in the big schoolroom that night. My mother heard there was a revival going on there, and she sent me to fetch my little brother away; she did not want him, she said, to get convinced; and I went to fetch my brother, and he was on his knees crying, Lord, have mercy upon me, a sinner. I stopped, and I prayed too, and the Lord saved us both.' "[6]

Spurgeon admitted that "God alone knows where that revival really begun. Some woman on her bed may have been exercised in her soul for that district, and may have been wrestling with God in prayer; and then the blessing descended."[7]

The closing prayer of his sermon is eminently suited for us today: "The Lord send to all the churches of Great Britain, first of all, the power of prayer, and then shall there come conversion of multitudes of souls through the outpoured energy of the Holy One of Israel."[8]

[5] *Ibid.*, 1860, p. 23.
[6] *Ibid.*
[7] *Ibid.*
[8] *Ibid.*, p. 24.

POSTSCRIPT

WHEREIN ARMINIAN AND CALVINIST AGREE

A Conversation between John Wesley and Charles Simeon

"Pray, sir, do you feel yourself a depraved creature, so depraved that you would never have thought of turning to God, if God had not first put it into your heart?"

"Yes," said the veteran Wesley, "I do, indeed."

"And do you utterly despair of recommending yourself to God by anything that you can do, and look for salvation solely through the blood and righteousness of Christ?"

"Yes, solely through Christ."

"But sir, supposing you were first saved by Christ, are you not, somehow or other, to save yourself afterwards by your own works,"

"No, I must be saved by Christ from first to last."

"Allowing, then, that you were first turned by the grace of God, are you not, in some way or other, to keep yourself by your own power?"

"No."

"What, then, are you to be upheld every hour and every moment by God, as much as an infant in its mother's arms?"

"Yes, altogether."

"And is all your hope in the grace and mercy of God to preserve you unto His heavenly kingdom?"

"Yes, I have no hope but in Him."

"Then, sir, with your leave, I will put up my dagger

again; *for this is all my Calvinism; this is my election, my justification by faith; my final perseverance; it is, in substance, all that I hold, and as I hold it."*

From The Hamilton Review,
Quoted in The Sword and the Trowel, 1886, p. 491.

www.ingramcontent.com/pod-product-compliance
Lightning Source LLC
Chambersburg PA
CBHW050829160426
43192CB00010B/1952